BLUEPRINTS
Technology
Key Stage 1

Tim Gadd

Dianne Morton

Stanley Thornes (Publishers) Ltd

BLUEPRINTS – HOW TO GET MORE INFORMATION

Blueprints is an expanding series of practical teacher's ideas books and photocopiable resources for use in primary schools. Books are available for every Key Stage of every core and foundation subject, as well as for an ever widening range of other primary needs. **Blueprints** are carefully structured around the demands of National Curriculum but may be used successfully by schools and teachers not following the National Curriculum in England and Wales.

Blueprints provide:

- Total National Curriculum coverage
- Hundreds of practical ideas
- Books specifically for the Key Stage you teach
- Flexible resources for the whole school or for individual teachers
- Excellent photocopiable sheets – ideal for assessment, SATs and children's work profiles
- Supreme value.

Books may be bought by credit card over the telephone and information obtained on (0242) 228888. Alternatively, photocopy and return this FREEPOST form to join our mailing list. We will mail you regularly with information on new and existing titles.

Photocopiable

Please add my name to the BLUEPRINTS mailing list.
Name _____
Address _____
_____
_____
Postcode _____
To: Marketing Services Dept., Stanley Thornes Publishers, FREEPOST (GR 782), Cheltenham, Glos. GL53 1BR

© Text Timothy Gadd and Dianne Morton 1992
© Illustrations ST(P) Ltd 1992

The copyright holders authorise ONLY purchasers of *Blueprints: Technology, Key Stage 1* to make photocopies or stencil duplicates of the record sheets for their own or their classes' immediate use within the teaching context.

No other rights are granted without prior permission in writing from the publisher or under licence from the Copyright Licensing Agency Limited. Further details of such licences (for reprographic reproduction) may be obtained from the Copyright Licensing Agency Limited, of 90 Tottenham Court Road, London W1P 9HE.

Copy by any other means or for any other purpose is strictly prohibited without the prior written consent of the copyright holders.

Applications for such permission should be addressed to the publishers:
Stanley Thornes (Publishers) Ltd, Ellenborough House, Wellington Street,
CHELTENHAM GL50 1YD, England

First published in 1992 by
Stanley Thornes (Publishers) Ltd
Ellenborough House
Wellington Street
CHELTENHAM GL50 1YD

Reprinted 1993

A catalogue record for this book is available from the British Library.

ISBN 07487–1357–3

Typeset by Tech-Set, Gateshead, Tyne & Wear.
Printed and bound in Great Britain at The Bath Press, Avon.

CONTENTS

Introduction	v
How to use this book	vi
Topic Planner	viii
Technology from Themes:	1
Movement	4
Changes	28
Taking care of things	43
Structures	57
Out and about	74
Technology from stories	90
Useful techniques and ideas	107
Challenges	119
Resource and records:	139
Checklist of classroom equipment and materials	140
Storage ideas	141
Designing	143
Technology Attainment Target record	145
Programmes of Study record	146

ACKNOWLEDGEMENT

The authors would like to thank the staff and children of Nook Lane Junior School and Holt House Infant School in Sheffield for all their help with this book.

INTRODUCTION

The aim of this book is to provide teachers of Key Stage 1 children with practical ways of tackling Technology in their classroom. It is linked throughout to National Curriculum requirements for Technology and the Attainment Targets and Programmes of Study for profile component 1: Design and Technology capability outlined in *Technology in the National Curriculum*. However, because of the universal nature of Technology it may be used equally effectively by teachers of children in the 5 to 7 age range outside England and Wales who are seeking ideas for Technology work.

Blueprints: Technology provides a large bank of ideas for Technology at Key Stage 1 plus photocopiable materials for use by teachers and children. The activities are based upon normal classroom practice with a strong emphasis on a thematic approach which allows Technology to be linked across the curriculum or through topic work, so that children always have the chance to carry out technological activities in meaningful contexts.

The book closely follows Key Stage 1 Technology in the National Curriculum and covers all the Attainment Targets and the entire content of the Programmes of Study for Design and Technology capability. It can thus meet individual teacher's requirements for National Curriculum Technology, as well as providing schemes of work for teachers throughout a school. It is arranged in the following five sections:

Technology from themes

This section is the most substantial part of the book. It provides an illustrated ideas bank for five key themes within which there are ten topics. Each topic may be used as part of a theme, or independently, providing flexibility to meet individual needs. Each topic includes a children's evaluation sheet.

Technology from stories

This section provides detailed suggestions for using infant story books as a basis for Technology work. There is also a bibliography of other stories that may be used in the same way.

Useful techniques and ideas

This provides a resource of basic techniques in key areas of Technology for infant children. The section focuses on frameworks and structures, wheels and axles, pulleys, cogs and gears, joining things and electrics. These techniques are referred to widely throughout the book.

Challenges

This is a free-standing bank of Challenges which Key Stage 1 children can undertake on their own. They can also be linked into topic work Technology in various ways.

Resources and records

This section provides useful checklists of tools and materials to use at Key Stage 1, practical photocopiable record-keeping sheets for National Curriculum work and ideas for storage of materials in the infant classroom.

Many of the photocopiable sheets are intended for teacher use, although there may be times when they can be used directly with children. Two sections of photocopiable sheets are intended specifically for children's use. These are the Evaluation Sheets that accompany each theme and the Challenges.

HOW TO USE THIS BOOK

Blueprints: Technology is an extremely flexible resource which can be used in many different ways to meet the needs of each class. It can also be used to provide a framework for Technology throughout the school.

Teachers may want to use the ideas in this book in one, or more, of the following ways:

1 Starting from themes

There are five broad themes covered in the section Technology from themes. They are:

Movement
Changes
Taking care of things
Structures
Out and about

They have been chosen to reflect the thematic approach taken by many infant schools. The themes provide realistic opportunities to build upon experiences familiar to children, and place Technology within the context of the whole curriculum.

Each theme can provide at least one full term's work if used in the ways suggested. Each one will enable children to cover all the Attainment Targets and the entire content of the Programmes of Study (Levels 1, 2, 3) at Key Stage 1. The themes provide a large number of topics, and within the book, ten of these are developed in detail, (two per theme). The topics have been carefully chosen to reflect a balance of the five contexts from the National Curriculum Programmes of Study. For example, for *Structures*, the following topics are suggested:

Houses	Swimming pool
Furniture	Roads and bridges
Garage	Fire station
Building materials	The Building Site
Keeping warm	Railway station
School garden	Bus station
The park	

Of these, Houses and The Building Site are developed in detail.

On page 3 a planning chart is provided. This gives an overview of all the themes, the topics they contain and the related contexts.

In order to set Technology within the context of the whole curriculum, a web is included for each theme that details work that could be developed in English, Science, Mathematics, History, Geography, Music Art, PE and RE:

Two topics are developed in detail for each theme. You will find an at-a-glance flow chart for each one that provides a route through the complete design process encompassing all the Attainment Targets. For example:

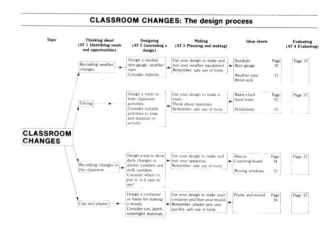

After each flow chart there is a set of Ideas Sheets and an Evaluation Sheet for children to complete.

To work from themes therefore, teachers should:
1 Select a theme. (Use its web to help identify cross-curricular potential).
2 Select a topic within that theme.
3 Turn to the flow chart that relates to that topic.
4 Follow the route through the chart from 'Thinking about' to 'Designing' to 'Planning and making' to 'Evaluating'. This will take children through the

vi

complete design process and all the Attainment Targets.
5 Use the Ideas Sheets for 'planning and making' activities.
6 Give the children an Evaluation Sheet, that will help them to reflect on their work. We suggest that these sheets are kept to form a record of the children's Technology work and as part of their Record of Achievement to share with parents.

2 Starting from topics

Teachers may want to use *Blueprints: Technology* to provide ideas for a wide range of topics. The following ten topics are contained within the themes:
Moving Toys
Vehicles
Classroom Changes
Changes around Us
Pets
The Playground
Houses
The Building Site
Direction Games
Holidays.

In addition the topic planner on page viii will show how you can use ideas across the book to resource a wider range of topics.

3 Starting from Programmes of Study

These can be approached through the contexts given in the National Curriculum document:
Home
School
Recreation
Community
Business and Industry
by following the format on page 3 where each of these contexts is considered through a range of familiar themes and topics.

Alternatively each complete theme covers the entire content of the Programmes of Study (Levels 1, 2, 3) at Key Stage 1:

- Satisfying needs and opportunities (covered in the 'Thinking about' column on each topic page)
- Developing and using artefacts, systems and environments
- Working with materials (covered in the 'Designing' and 'Planning and making' process)
- Developing and communicating ideas (covered in both the 'Planning' and the 'Evaluating' process within each topic).

Teachers can therefore feel confident of meeting the requirements of the Programmes of Study by following their chosen theme and topics. Page 146 gives a check-list for teachers to record their Programmes of Study coverage as they plan their work for the term.

4 Starting from Attainment Targets

Teachers who wish to approach Technology through Attainment Targets, can do this by working with the themes in the book.
Each topic addresses the four Attainment Targets:
AT 1 Identifying needs and opportunities
AT 2 Generating a design
AT 3 Planning and making
AT 4 Evaluating
from 'Thinking about' to 'Designing' to 'Making' and finally to 'Evaluating'.

Children will work through the Attainment Targets at their own appropriate level and a record sheet for teachers to monitor each child's progress is given on page 145.

5 Starting from stories

Stories are an essential part of school life and as such, provide an excellent vehicle for Technology that is automatically stimulating and interesting to children.

In this section, eight familiar stories for 5–7 year olds have been selected to show how Technology can be developed from stories. The section makes use of techniques and materials that the children will have met elsewhere in the book. These are merely suggestions and it is hoped that both teachers and children will find further possibilities for Technology for themselves. The stories may also be linked into some topics through the topic planner on page viii.

6 Starting from challenges

This section is a free-standing resource of individual Challenges for children to undertake on their own, in pairs or in groups.

TOPIC PLANNER

As well as the section Technology from Themes, which provides specific themes and topics for Technology, there are many other ideas and activities in this book which can be used to resource a wide range of popular Key Stage 1 topics. This planner will enable you to locate activities in the book to use within a wider topic framework.

Houses, homes and buildings

Technology from Themes ideas sheets: 5-6 Cranes (for building sites); 30 Model pet's home; 32 Small pets' beds; 33 Large pet's beds; 38 Bird feeders and nest box; The Houses topic (Ideas sheets 39-46); The Building Site topic (Ideas sheets 47-50); 51 Caravans 1; 61 3-D features.

Technology from stories: 1 Tumbledown (a church, a bridge, a village hall); 2 The Cow who fell in the Canal (a windmill); 3 The Mice and the Clockwork Bus (a shoe house); 4 I don't want to live in a House (a tent, an igloo, a tree house, a cave); 5 Phoebe and her Hot-Water Bottles (a bed); 7 Kit and the Magic Kite (a witch's house).

Challenges: 5 Can you make a wigwam? 12 Can you make a bridge? 17 Can you make a tower?

Useful techniques and ideas: 1 and 2 Basic frameworks (for making all kinds of model buildings); 8 Using simple pulleys (a windmill); 11 Electricity (lighting model houses).

Weather

Technology from Themes ideas sheets: 20 Sundials and Rain gauge; 21 Weather-vane and Windsock.

Pets and animals

Technology from Themes ideas sheets: 11 Finger puppets; 15 Hinged and pull toys; 16 Mobiles; The Pets topic (Ideas sheets 30-33); 37 Bird tables; 38 Bird feeders and Nest box; 54 Roundabout.

Technology from Stories: 3 The Mice and the Clockwork Bus; 7 Kit and the Magic Kite; 8 The Enormous Crocodile.

Travel, transport and roads

Technology from Themes ideas sheets: The Vehicles topic (Ideas sheets 1-9); 13 Hot air balloon and Parachutes; 27 Traffic lights; 45 Garages; 49 Bulldozer and Road roller; 51 Caravans; 55 Kite.

Technology from stories: 1 Tumbledown (a bridge); 2 The Cow who fell in the Canal (a waggon, raft and bridge); 3 The Mice and the Clockwork Bus (a bus); 4 I don't want to live in a House (a raft); 5 Phoebe and her Hot-Water Bottles (a trolley).

Challenges: 3 Can you make a vehicle with wobbly wheels? 12 Can you make a bridge to stretch between two tables? 19 Can you make a model shopping trolley?

Useful techniques and ideas: 1 and 2 Basic frameworks (for making vehicle frames); 3 Wheels; 4 Giving grip to wheels; 5 Spacers and end stops for axles; 6 Fastening wheels and axles to a chassis.

Movement

Technology from Themes ideas sheets: The Vehicles topic (Ideas sheets 1-9); 13 Hot air balloon and Parachutes; 16 Mobiles; 17 Zoetrope; 18 Kaleidoscope; 19 Flick book; 23 Pendulums; 25 Moving windows; 34 Model playground equipment; 54 Roundabout; 57 Spinners.

Technology from stories: 3 The Mice and the Clockwork Bus; 4 I don't want to live in a House (a raft); 5 Phoebe and her Hot-Water Bottles (a trolley); 8 The Enormous Crocodile (a fairground).

Challenges: Can you make a Jack-in-the-Box? 15 Can you make a face with moving parts? 19 Can you make a model shopping trolley?

Useful techniques and ideas: 3 Wheels; 4 Giving grip to wheels; 5 Spacers and end stops for axles; 6 Fastening wheels and axles to a chassis; 7 Simple pulleys; 8 Using simple pulleys.

Food and farms

Technology and Themes ideas sheets: 9 Easy-to-make vehicles 3; 61 3-D Features.

Technology from stories: 2 The Cow who fell in the Canal (a windmill, a cheese carrier and scales, a gate); 6 The Giant Jam Sandwich (a loaf, a bread transporter).

Useful techniques and ideas: 1 and 2 Basic frameworks (for making model farm buildings); 8 Using simple pulleys (a windmill).

Plants and trees

Technology from Themes ideas sheets: 36 Flower and plant tubs.

Air and flight

Technology from Themes ideas sheets: 13 Hot air balloon and Parachutes; 14 Planes; 21 Weather-vane and Windsock; 37 Bird tables; 38 Bird feeders and Nest box; 55 Kite; 56 Boats (balloon power).

Technology from stories: 6 The Giant Jam Sandwich (a flying machine).

Challenges: 1 Can you make a Jack-in-the-box? (pneumatic power).

Change

Technology from Themes ideas sheets: Classroom changes topic (Ideas sheets 20–26); Changes around us topic (Ideas sheets 27–29).

Water and ships

Technology from Themes ideas sheets: 20 Rain gauge; 22 Water-clock; 28 Lighthouse; 56 Boats.

Technology from stories: 2 The Cow who fell in the Canal (a raft); 4 I don't want to live in a House (a raft); 7 Kit and the Magic Kite (a boat).

Challenges: 1 Can you make a Jack-in-the-box? (Hydraulic power).

Useful techniques and ideas: 1 and 2 Basic frameworks (for making ship structures).

Clothes

Technology from Themes ideas sheets: 47 Hard hat and Safety clothes; 52 Sun-hats.

Time

Technology from Themes ideas sheets: 20 Sundials; 22 Water-clock and Sand-timer; 23 Pendulums.

Sound and music

Technology from Themes ideas sheets: 28 Lighthouse and Bells and buzzers.

Challenges: 13 Can you make a musical instrument with strings?

Colour and shape

Technology from Themes ideas sheets: 10 Shadow puppets; 18 Kaleidoscope; 19 Flick book; 27 Traffic lights; 26 Frame and mould; 41–42 Wallpaper design 1 and 2.

Challenges: 9 Can you make a robot with eyes that light up? Can you make a football stadium with lights?

Useful techniques and ideas: 11 Electricity.

School

Technology from Themes ideas sheets: The Playground topic (Ideas sheets 47–55).

Challenges: 14 Can you make a container for pencils, crayons etc? 16 Can you make a school sign?

Toys and games

Technology from Themes ideas sheets: The Moving Toys topic (Ideas sheets 10–19); 34 Model playground equipment; 35 Large playground games; 44 Toy box and containers; 45 Garages; 55 Kite; 56 Boat; The Direction Games topic (Ideas sheet 57–61).

Challenges: 1 Can you make a Jack-in-the-box? 7 Can you make a table game with a track that uses two dice? 8 Can you make a puppet theatre? 9 Can you make a robot with eyes that light up? 10 Can you make a football stadium with lights? 11 Can you make a baby's rattle? 15 Can you make a face with moving parts? 18 Can you make an alphabet mobile?

Puppets

Technology from Themes ideas sheets: 10 Shadow puppets; 11 Finger puppets and Glove puppets; 12 String puppets; 15 Hinged and pull toys.

Challenges: 8 Can you make a puppet theatre? 15 Can you make a face with moving parts?

Shops

Technology from Themes ideas sheets: 24 Abacus and Counting board.

Technology from stories: 2 The Cow who fell in the Canal (a market stall and weighing scales); 5 Phoebe and her Hot-Water Bottles (a shop).

Challenges: 2 Can you make a money box? 19 Can you make a model shopping trolley?

Useful techniques and ideas: 1 and 2 Basic frameworks (for model shops).

Signs and symbols

Technology from Themes ideas sheets: 27 Traffic lights; 28 Lighthouse and Bells and buzzers; 29 2-D and 3-D signs.

Challenges: 16 Can you make a school sign? 18 Can you make an alphabet mobile?

Energy

Technology from Themes ideas sheets: 1 and 2 Tip-up lorries; 3 Tractor and trailer and Power-driven vehicles; 5 and 6 Cranes; 7 and 8 Easy-to-make vehicles; 56 Boats.

Technology from stories: 2 The Cow who fell in the Canal (a windmill).

Machines

Technology from Themes ideas sheets: The Vehicles topic (Ideas sheet 1–9); 13 Hot air balloon; 41 Bulldozer and Road roller; 56 Boats.

Technology from stories: 2 The Cow who fell in the Canal (a windmill).

Challenges: 1 Can you make a Jack-in-the-box? 3 Can you make a vehicle with wobbly wheels? 4 Can you make a crane?

Useful techniques and ideas: 1 and 2 Basic frameworks (for frameworks for all kinds of machines); 7 Simple pulleys; 8 Using simple pulleys; 9 Cogs and gears.

> Topic planner

Structures

Technology from Themes ideas sheets: 39 Roofs; 50 Scaffolding.

Challenges: 4 Can you make a crane? 5 Can you make a wigwam? 12 Can you make a bridge? 17 Can you make a tower?

Environment

Technology from Themes ideas sheets: 37 Litter bins and Bird tables; 38 Bird feeders and Nest box.

Leisure

Technology from Themes ideas sheets: 31 Pets' playground; The Playground topic (Ideas sheets 34–38); The holiday topic (Ideas sheets 51–56).

Technology from stories: 8 The Enormous Crocodile (a fairground).

Challenges: 7 Can you make a table game with a track that uses two dice?

Counting and numbers

Technology from Themes ideas sheets: 24 Abacus and Counting board; 25 Moving windows; 35 Large playground games; 57 Spinners; 58 3-D counters; 59 Dice.

Challenges: 7 Can you make a table game with a track that uses two dice?

Technology from themes

Five key themes are developed in this section of the book. They are: Movement; Changes; Taking care of things; Structures; Out and about. Each theme can provide work across all five of the Programme of Study contexts set out in the chart on page 3 'Planning technology from themes'. You will see here that we have suggested topics that will serve each theme. The two in bold in each column have been treated in detail and form the ideas bank from that theme. For example the Movement theme concentrates on Moving Toys and Vehicles but lists other topics that could be covered. (Ideas about other topics can be accessed from the topic planner on page viii.

Each theme can provide at least one full term's work if used in the ways suggested. You will find that the theme starts with a planning web outlining ideas for Technology. The web also relates Technology to the wider curriculum.

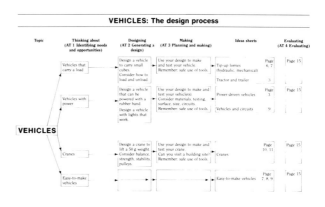

This chart demonstrates the design process cycle which can be illustrated as follows:

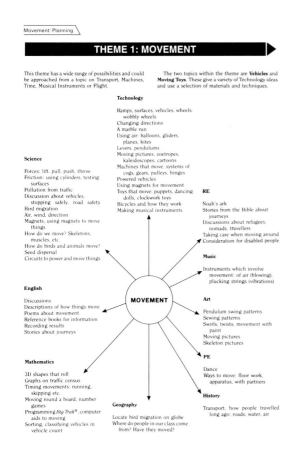

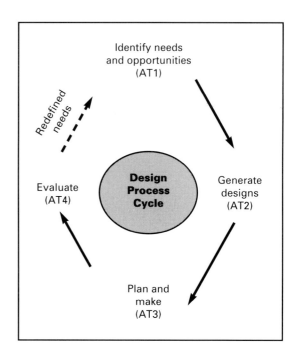

The theme shows how you can use the two topics provided in detail. Each topic in the theme is introduced by a chart showing you how to follow it through all the ATs. You will then have covered the complete design process, from 'Thinking About' (AT1) through to 'Evaluating' (AT4).

In order to help children with the designing process, there is information and a photocopiable design sheet in the Resources and Records section at the back of the book. (See pages 139–149.) The main focus is upon AT3 (Making) and we have provided many ideas sheets, to give suggestions for planning and making model vehicles. This ideas bank is intended to be used flexibly by you with the children, rather than to be made up as recipes. At the end of each topic you will find an evaluation sheet, intended to be used directly by children to structure their own thinking about what happened.

Here is the evaluation sheet for vehicles:

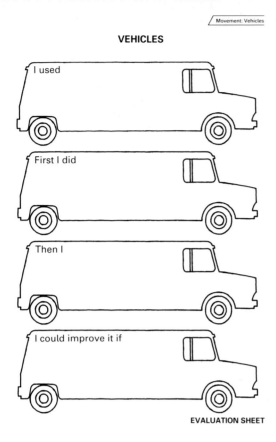

These sheets can be used to record work on any activity related to the topic and can usefully be kept to form a record of Technology work. Further suggestions about using this Themes section can be found in 'How to use this book'.

PLANNING TECHNOLOGY FROM THEMES

Themes and topics / Programme of Study context	Movement	Changes	Taking care of things	Structures	Out and about
Home	Machines in the home Systems Clocks	Cooking and baking Heating and freezing Effect of water	**Pets** Things around the house	**Houses** Furniture Garage	In the garden Clothes
School	Table games Playground toys	Shapes and puzzles **Classroom Changes** Improving models	Storing things Safety in school A friendly school	Building materials Keeping warm School garden	**Direction Games** Travelling to school
Recreation	**Moving Toys** Musical instruments	Indoor gardens Toys that change	**The Playground** Playground activities	The park Swimming pool	**Holidays** The fair The circus
Community	**Vehicles** Mobility for the disabled	Recycling **Changes around Us** Changing lifestyles	Shopping Caring for babies	Roads and bridges Fire station	Trains and tracks Shops
Business and industry	Transport Cranes Machines old and new	Materials Waterproofing	Saving money	**The Building Site** Railway station Bus station	Boats and barges Air and aeroplanes

Movement: Planning

THEME 1: MOVEMENT

This theme has a wide range of possibilities and could be approached from a topic on Transport, Machines, Time, Musical Instruments or Flight.

The two topics within the theme are **Vehicles** and **Moving Toys**. These give a variety of Technology ideas and use a selection of materials and techniques.

Technology

Ramps, surfaces, vehicles, wheels, wobbly wheels
Changing directions
A marble run
Using air: balloons, gliders, planes, kites
Levers, pendulums
Moving pictures, zoetropes, kaleidoscopes, cartoons
Machines that move, systems of cogs, gears, pulleys, hinges
Powered vehicles
Using magnets for movement
Toys that move: puppets, dancing dolls, clockwork toys
Bicycles and how they work
Making musical instruments

Science

Forces: lift, pull, push, throw
Friction: using cylinders, testing surfaces
Pollution from traffic
Discussion about vehicles, stopping safely, road safety
Bird migration
Air, wind, direction
Magnets, using magnets to move things
How do we move? Skeletons, muscles, etc.
How do birds and animals move?
Seed dispersal
Circuits to power and move things

RE

Noah's ark
Stories from the Bible about journeys
Discussions about refugees, nomads, travellers
Taking care when moving around
Consideration for disabled people

Music

Instruments which involve movement: of air (blowing), plucking strings (vibrations)

English

Discussions
Descriptions of how things move
Poems about movement
Reference books for information
Recording results
Stories about journeys

MOVEMENT

Art

Pendulum swing patterns
Sewing patterns
Swirls, twists, movement with paint
Moving pictures
Skeleton pictures

PE

Dance
Ways to move: floor work, apparatus, with partners

Mathematics

3D shapes that roll
Graphs on traffic census
Timing movements: running, skipping etc.
Moving round a board, number games
Programming *Big Trak*®, computer aids to moving
Sorting, classifying vehicles in vehicle count

Geography

Locate bird migration on globe
Where do people in our class come from? Have they moved?

History

Transport, how people travelled long ago: roads, water, air

4

VEHICLES: The design process

Movement: Vehicles

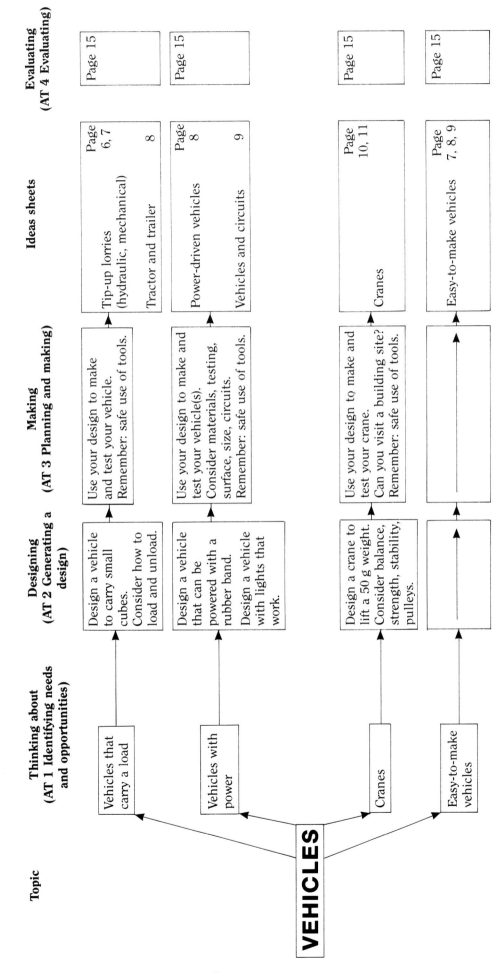

Movement: Vehicles

Tip-up lorries 1

Hydraulic tip-up

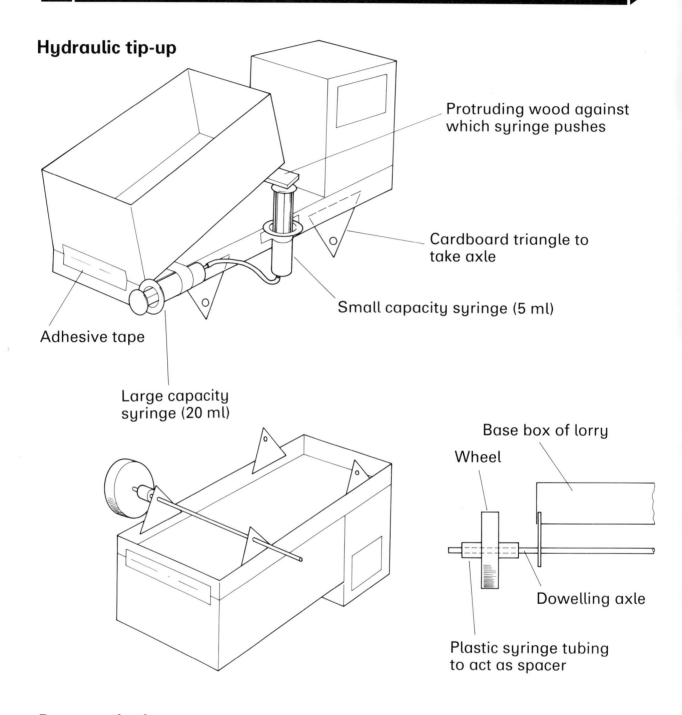

Pneumatic tip-up

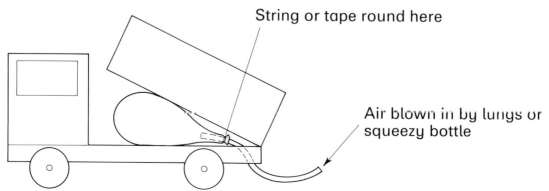

Movement: Vehicles

Tip-up lorries 2

Hand-tipped lorry

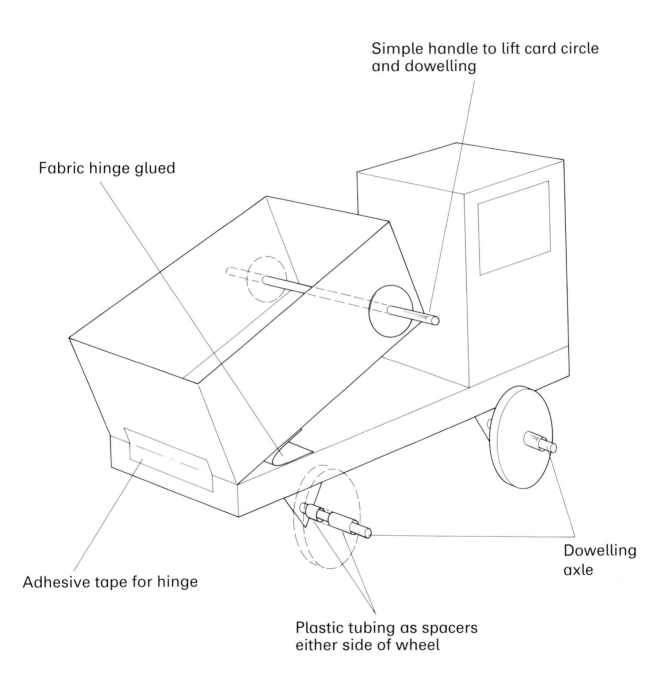

Movement: Vehicles

Ideas sheet 3: Tractor and trailer and power driven vehicle

Tractor and trailer

Power-driven vehicle

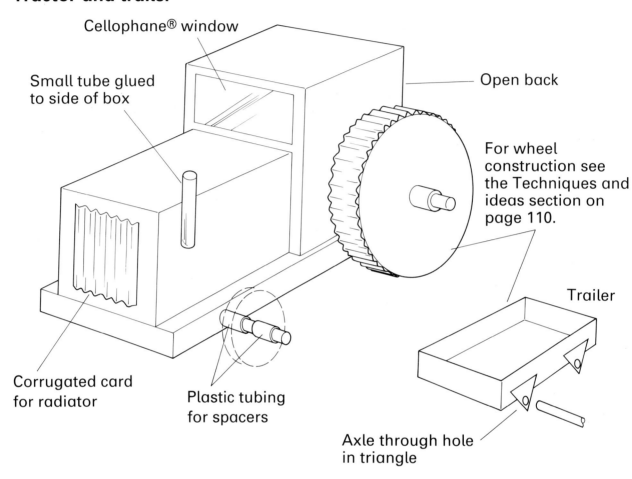

Movement: Vehicles

Vehicles and circuits

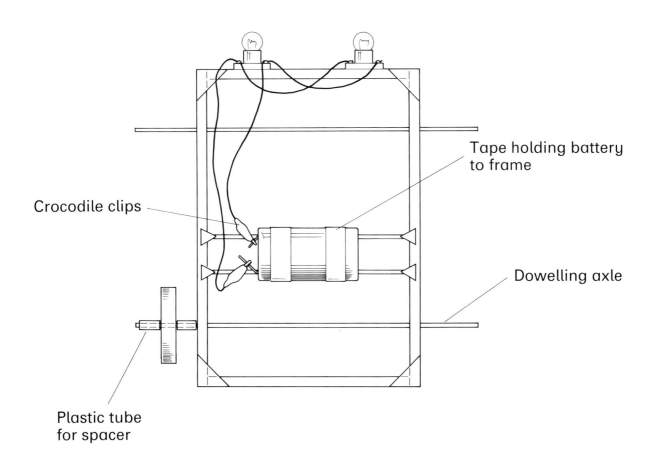

- Crocodile clips
- Tape holding battery to frame
- Dowelling axle
- Plastic tube for spacer

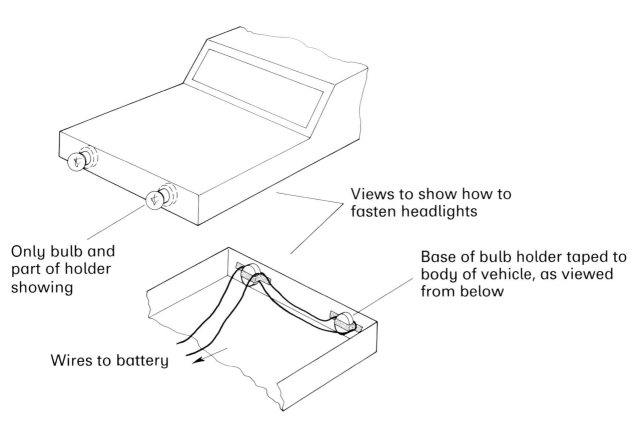

- Only bulb and part of holder showing
- Views to show how to fasten headlights
- Base of bulb holder taped to body of vehicle, as viewed from below
- Wires to battery

Movement: Vehicles

Cranes 1

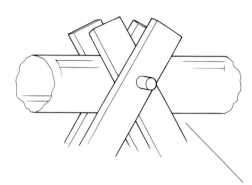

Wood drilled and dowelling pushed through

Tube as arm of crane

Strips of wood

Plastic tube

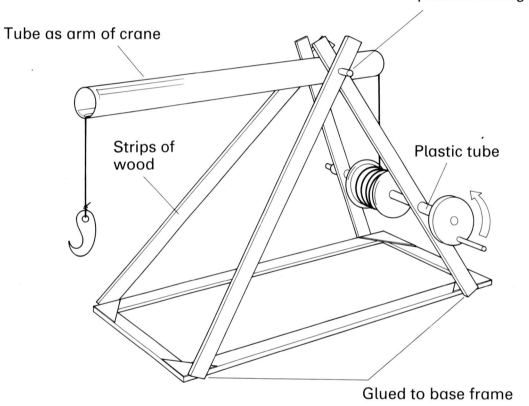

Glued to base frame

Pulley wheel (bobbin)

Wooden wheel or stiff card

Plastic tubing as a 'stop'

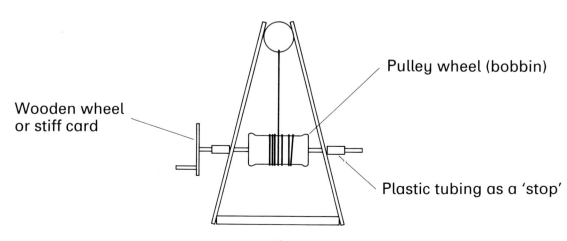

Movement: Vehicles

Cranes 2

Ideas sheet 6

1

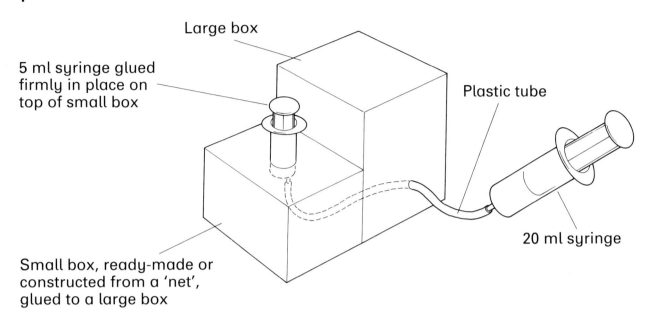

- Large box
- 5 ml syringe glued firmly in place on top of small box
- Plastic tube
- 20 ml syringe
- Small box, ready-made or constructed from a 'net', glued to a large box

2

- Glued to frame
- String with hook at end tied to arm
- Wooden frame with long arm fastened to it

3

- Tape acts as hinge

4

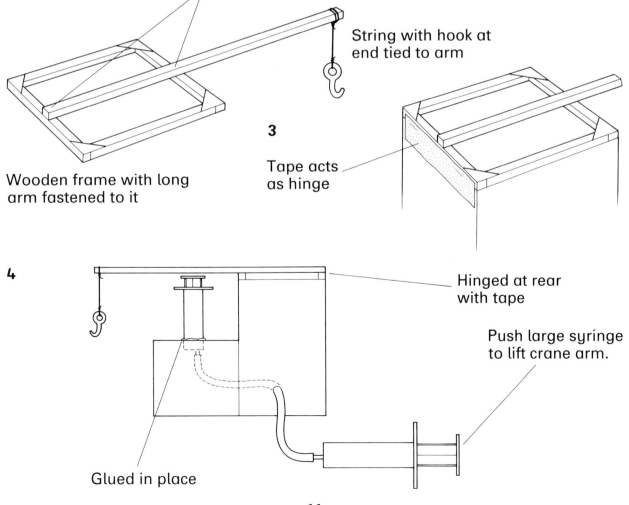

- Hinged at rear with tape
- Push large syringe to lift crane arm.
- Glued in place

Movement: Vehicles

Easy-to-make vehicles 1

Cotton reel vehicles

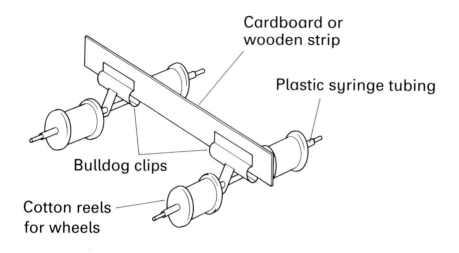

Simple-wheeled vehicle

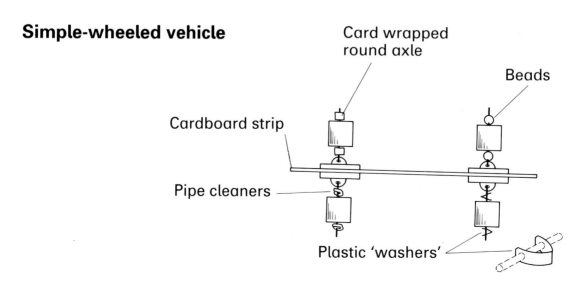

Ideas sheet 8

Movement: Vehicles

Easy-to-make vehicles 2

Bicycle

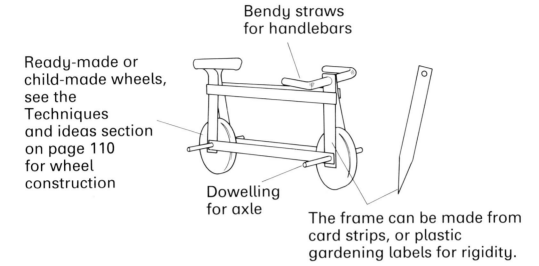

Ready-made or child-made wheels, see the Techniques and ideas section on page 110 for wheel construction

Bendy straws for handlebars

Dowelling for axle

The frame can be made from card strips, or plastic gardening labels for rigidity.

Peg vehicle

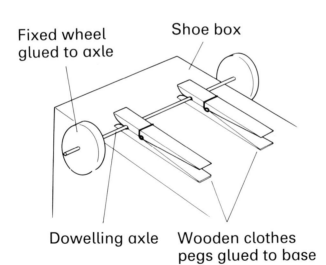

Fixed wheel glued to axle

Shoe box

Dowelling axle

Wooden clothes pegs glued to base

Marble vehicle

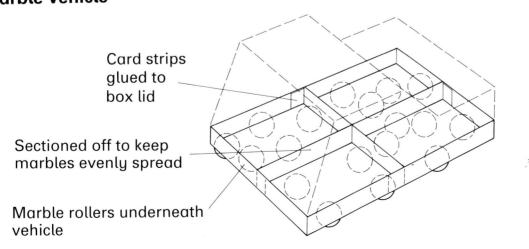

Card strips glued to box lid

Sectioned off to keep marbles evenly spread

Marble rollers underneath vehicle

13

Movement: Vehicles

Easy-to-make vehicles 3

Elastic-powered roller

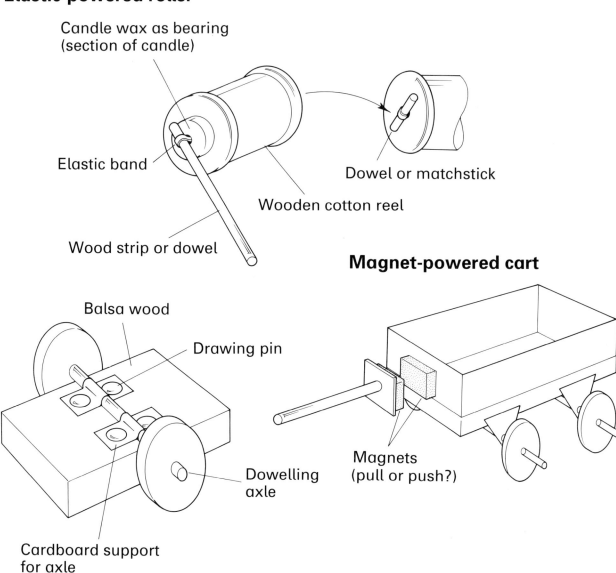

Magnet-powered cart

Wheelbarrow

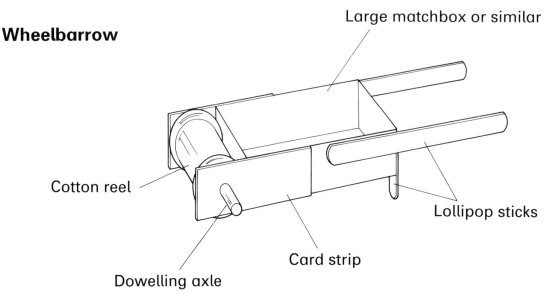

Movement: Vehicles

VEHICLES

EVALUATION SHEET

Movement: Moving toys

MOVING TOYS: The design process

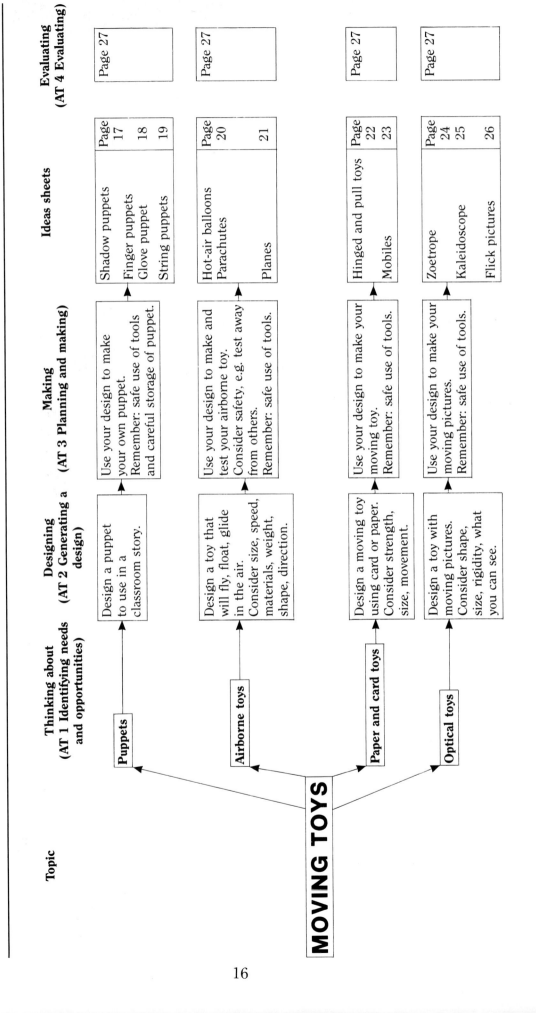

Movement: Moving toys

Shadow puppets

Ideas sheet 10

Ask children to draw their own or their friends' shadows in different poses to help them become familiar with the various body positions.

1 Design body shapes using card.

2 Cut out and fasten to a handle using dowelling or straw.

3 Think carefully about where to fasten the handle.

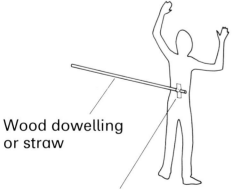

Wood dowelling or straw

Secure with adhesive tape or glue.

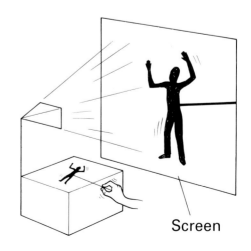

Screen

17

Movement: Moving toys

Ideas sheet 11: Finger puppets and glove puppet

Finger puppets

1 Draw round two fingers to make sure your puppet is big enough.

2 Design your character.

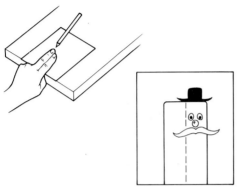

3 Re-create your design using felt or other material.

Cut-out features stitched or glued on

4 Join and glue or stitch.

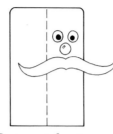
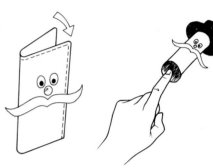

Make a mouse.

1 Approx. 6 cm radius semi-circle of suitable material, i.e. felt or thin card

2 Roll and fold to make a cone shape. Glue or stitch together.

3 Add features and fasten them on.

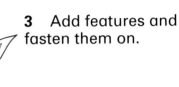
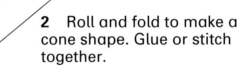

Glove puppet

1 Draw round your hand and cut out two pieces of material.

2 Design a character and cut out features. Fasten on with glue (or stitch).

Leave plenty of room.

Material

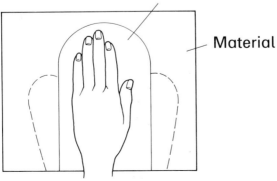
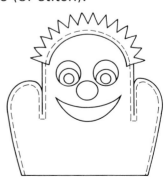

3 Stitch on dotted line and insert hand.

18

String puppets

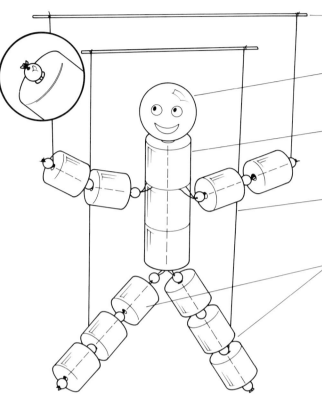

Dowelling

Ping-pong or polystyrene ball

Fasten the 'body' tightly together.

String

Fasten together with string and beads to allow movement.

Connect the arms and legs with string threaded though the centre holes. Use beads for spacers.

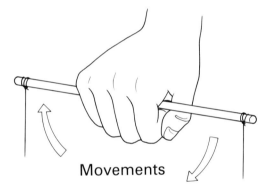

Movements

Lifting and lowering causes puppet to move, i.e. dance or walk.

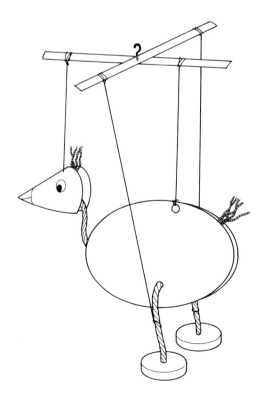

Close-up

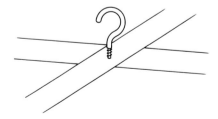

Movement: Moving toys

Hot-air balloon and parachutes

Hot-air balloon

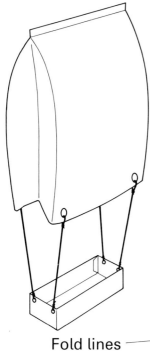

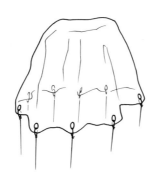

Use a thin paper bag or a small lightweight plastic bag.

4 Fasten the basket to the strings.

5 Inflate the balloon with warm air from a hair dryer.

1 Make holes in the corners or all around the bag.

2 Cut strings (from fine thread) to support the basket and secure to the balloon.

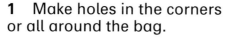

Fold lines

Tabs to glue

3 Make the basket from a 'net'. Remember to leave tabs to glue together.

Parachutes

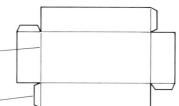

Polythene or other material

Punch holes in the corner for the string.

Strings the same length

Weight

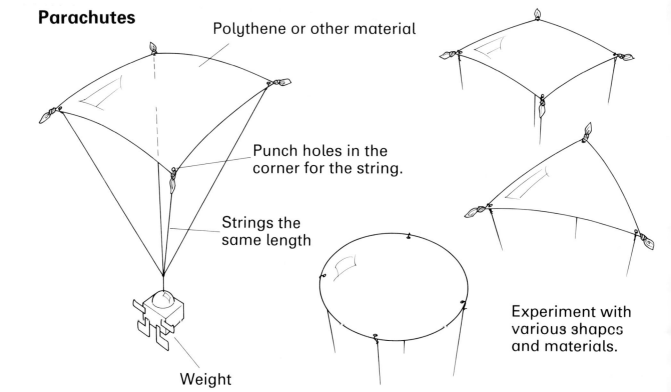

Experiment with various shapes and materials.

20

Movement: Moving toys

Planes

1 Fold in half.

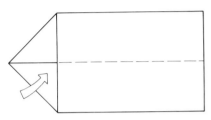

2 Open out.

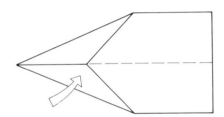

3 Fold the corners.

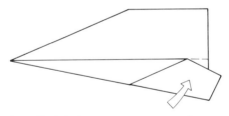

4 Fold the corners again.

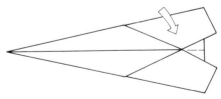

5 Fold the outside edges to the centre.

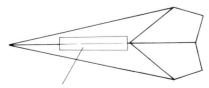

6 Fasten the edges together.

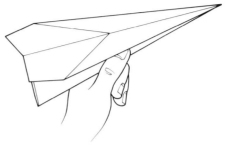

7 Launch the plane.

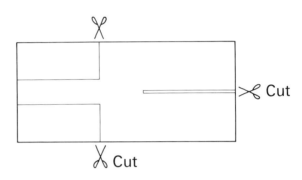

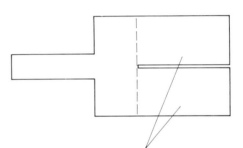

Fold in opposite directions.

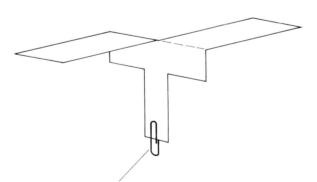

Paper clip for weight

Experiment with different sizes, shapes and weights.

Movement: Moving toys

Hinged and pull toys

Clown

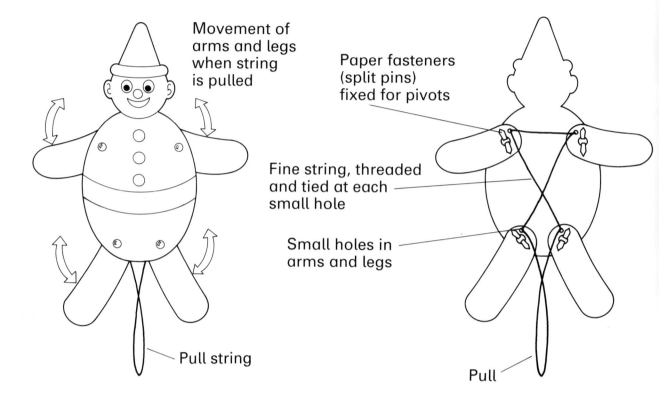

Owl

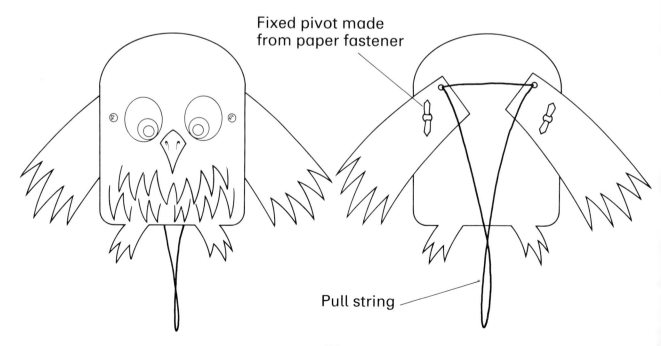

Movement: Moving toys

Mobiles

Ideas sheet 16

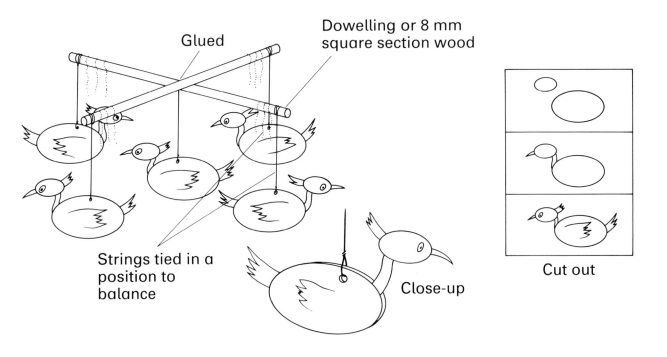

Glued
Dowelling or 8 mm square section wood
Strings tied in a position to balance
Close-up
Cut out

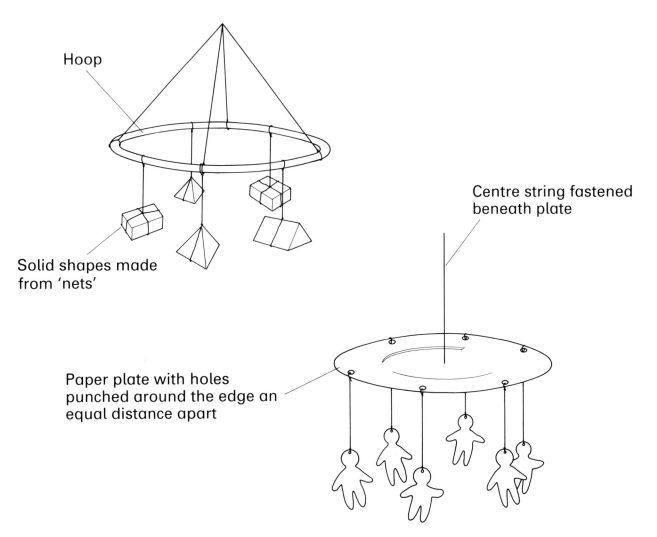

Hoop
Solid shapes made from 'nets'
Centre string fastened beneath plate
Paper plate with holes punched around the edge an equal distance apart

23

Movement: Moving toys

Zoetrope

Ideas sheet 17

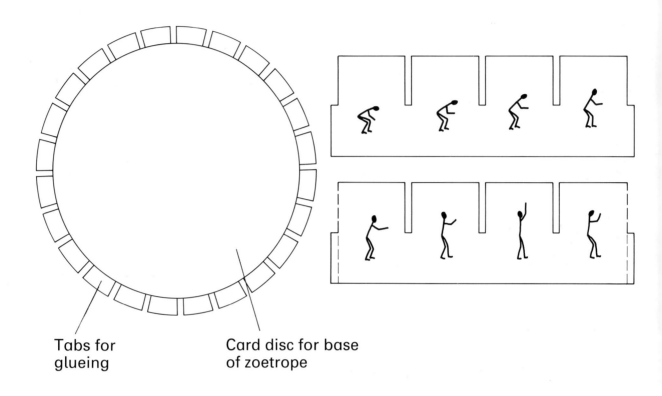

Tabs for glueing

Card disc for base of zoetrope

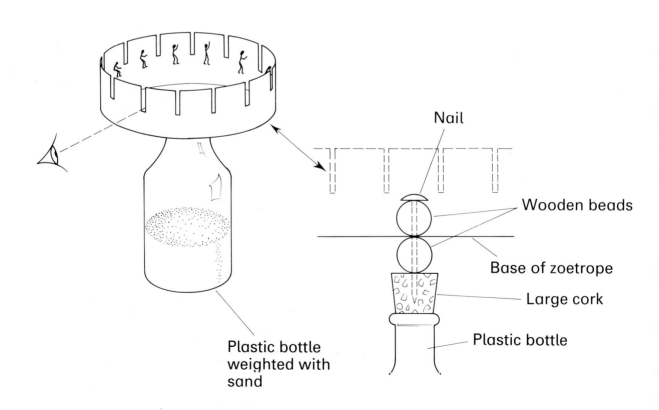

Plastic bottle weighted with sand

Nail

Wooden beads

Base of zoetrope

Large cork

Plastic bottle

Movement: Moving toys

Kaleidoscope

1. You will need a cylinder of cardboard. You can make one or use a ready-made box or tube.

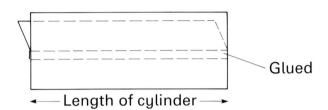

Glued

←— Length of cylinder —→

2. Card to fit into cylinder. Use shiny or reflective card for best results.

3. Fold to make a Y-shaped profile and insert into cylinder.

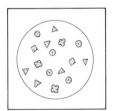 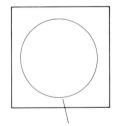

Draw circles the same size as cylinder onto two pieces of grease-proof paper.

4. You need coloured shapes such as sequins. Glue carefully round the edges of the circles and place together trapping the sequins between the circles in a 'sandwich'.

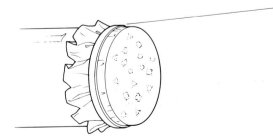

5. Use an elastic band to fasten the double layer of grease-proof paper to the tube.

6. Hold to light and look down the tube to see the colours. Rotate the tube.

Movement: Moving toys

Flick book

String threaded through holes and tied tightly

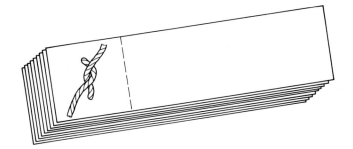

1   You need to draw a series of small pictures with each one being very slightly different from the last.

2   When you have completed this, cut your sheet into small 'pages' and fasten together as shown.

3   Hold the flick book in your left hand (between finger and thumb) and flick the pages with right thumb.

Movement: Moving toys

MOVING TOYS

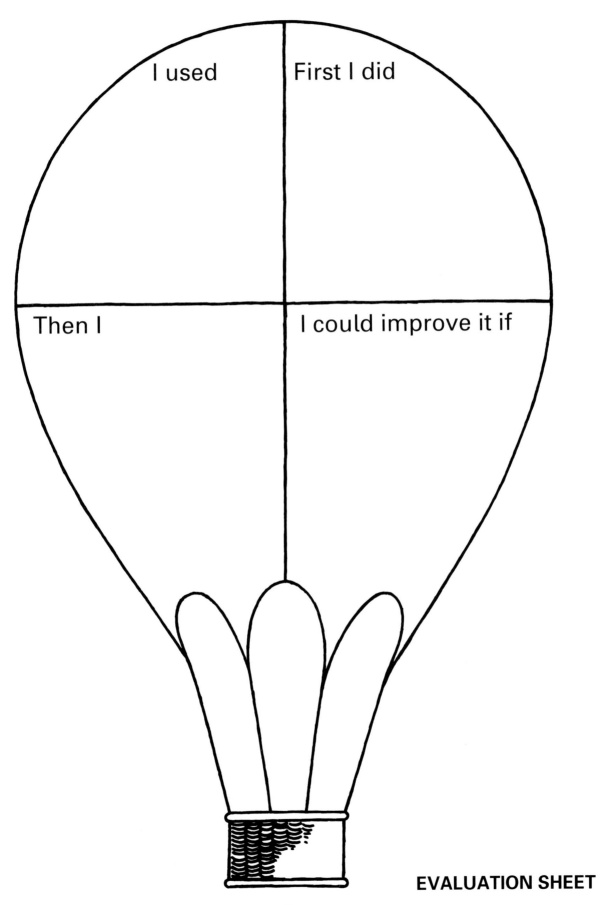

EVALUATION SHEET

Changes: Planning

THEME 2: CHANGES

This broad theme relates well to many science-based topics and opens up possibilities for cooking and Home Economics activities. It could be approached through a Recycling topic such as Investigating Materials, A Study of Gardens and Growth or even as part of a wider topic on Water. The topics developed in detail are **Classroom Changes** and **Changes around us**.

Science

Insects, life cycles, frogs, butterflies
Evolution, dinosaurs
Seasonal changes, weather, temperature
Growing plants and recording change, e.g. beans, tomatoes, seeds
Change and decay of fruit and other foods
Erosion, effects of weathering on the local environment
Waterproofing
Rust, effect of water

English

Discussion of observations
Recording observations
Writing poems about young and old
Descriptions of old and young people, of historical events
Sharing storybooks, reading stories about Change (e.g. The Shrinking of Treehorn)
Imaginary stories

Mathematics

Number patterns, adding 10, multiplication functions
Calculators, function machines
Shape: 2D and 3D, patterns and nets
Logic games
Data collection, recording observed changes in science

Technology

Cooking: heating and cooling, effect of cooking on food (eggs, cakes, puddings etc.)
Changing shapes, constructing 3-D shapes
Materials that change: sand, plaster, clay, *Modroc*®
Effect of glues and varnish
Changing models to improve or adapt, the evaluation process
Making things that change: traffic lights, flashing lighthouse
Making things to warn of changes, e.g. signs, buzzers, sending messages, timing devices for school activities
Recording changes, making systems to use in school, e.g. milk numbers, dinner numbers
Recycling, making newspaper, using junk and models

Geography

Changing direction, pathways and routes

Art

Changing shapes, repeating patterns, symmetry, Esher's work
Clay, making moulds
Tie-dye
Marbling
Shade and tone
Colour mixing

RE

Growing up
Growing old
Caring
Changing life styles, moving house, moving country

Music

Changing beat and rhythm
Stringed instruments: length of string related to sound
Milk bottle instruments: change depth of water to change sound

PE

Balancing/changing body parts
Dance and drama

History

My family (back to grandparents)
How people change
How life changes, e.g. domestic items
Buildings

Changes: Classroom changes

CLASSROOM CHANGES: The design process

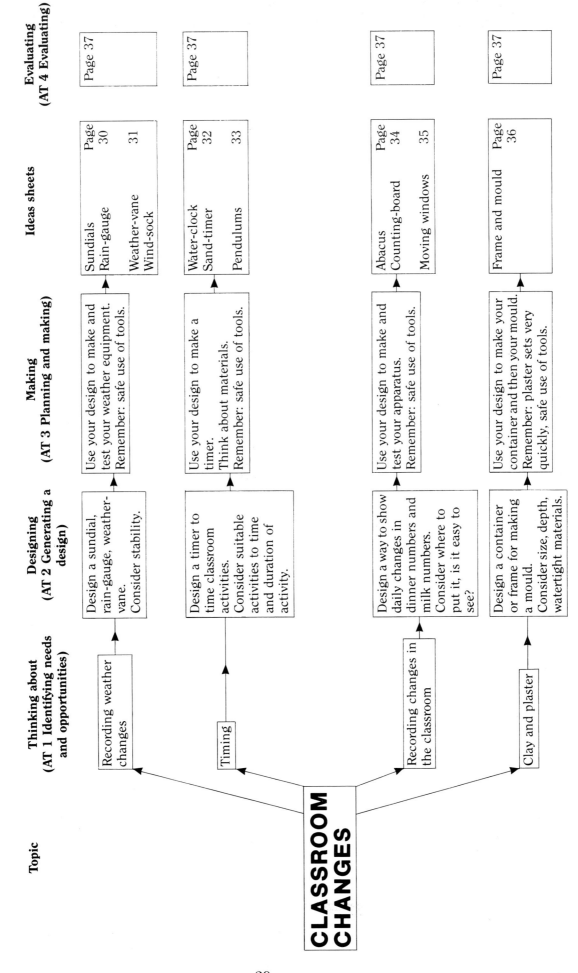

Changes: Classroom changes

Sundials and rain-gauge

Sundials

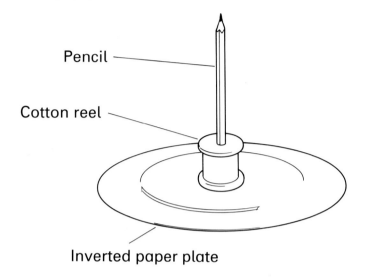

Pencil
Cotton reel
Inverted paper plate

Mark the shadow cast at regular intervals.

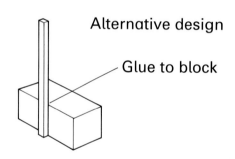

Alternative design
Glue to block

Rain-gauge

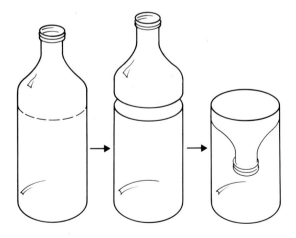

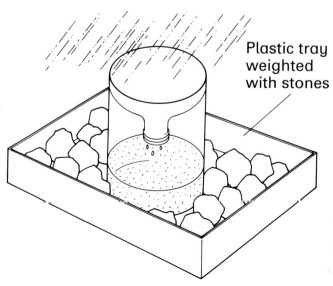

Plastic tray weighted with stones

Children can calibrate the gauge as often as required.

Weather-vane and wind-sock

Changes: Classroom changes

Weather-vane

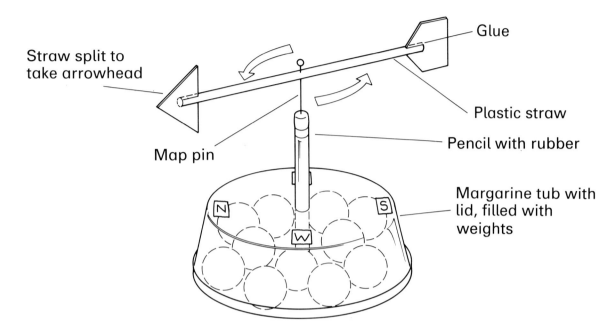

Wind-sock

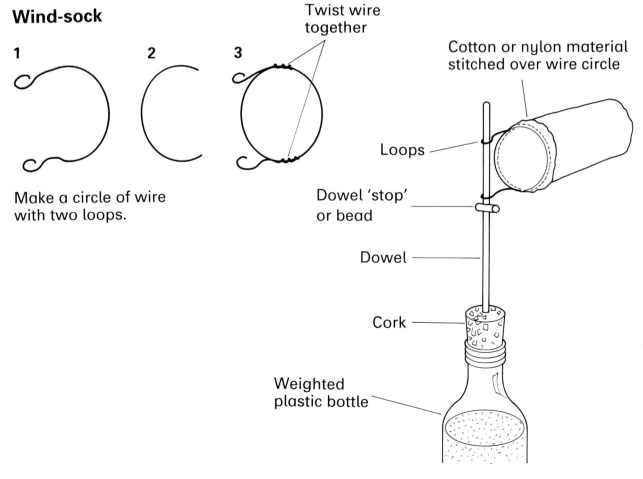

Make a circle of wire with two loops.

Changes: Classroom changes

Ideas sheet 22

Water-clock and sand-timer

Water-clock

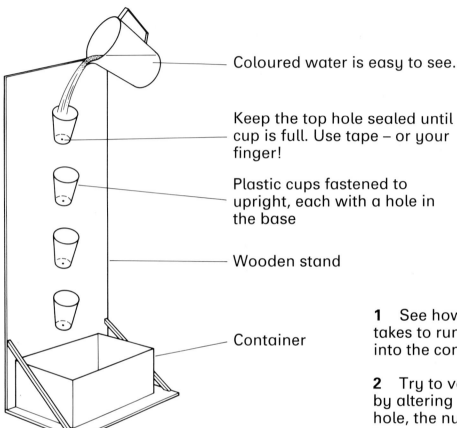

- Coloured water is easy to see.
- Keep the top hole sealed until cup is full. Use tape – or your finger!
- Plastic cups fastened to upright, each with a hole in the base
- Wooden stand
- Container

1 See how long the water takes to run through each cup into the container.

2 Try to vary the time taken by altering the size of the hole, the number of cups and the amount of water.

Sand-timer

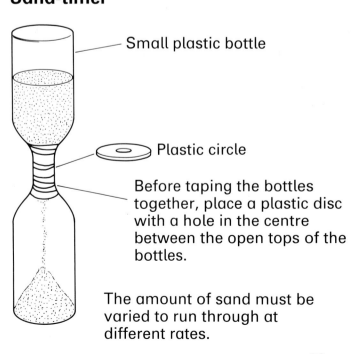

- Small plastic bottle
- Plastic circle
- Before taping the bottles together, place a plastic disc with a hole in the centre between the open tops of the bottles.
- The amount of sand must be varied to run through at different rates.

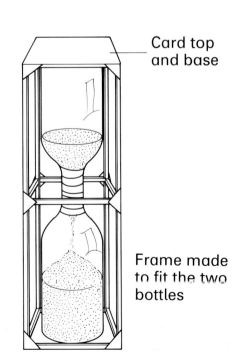

- Card top and base
- Frame made to fit the two bottles

Pendulums

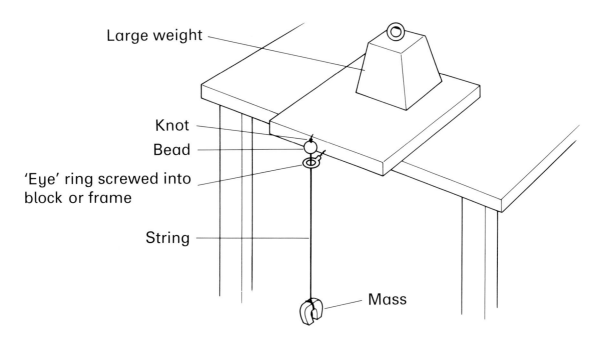

The time taken to stop swinging will vary according to the mass or the length of string.

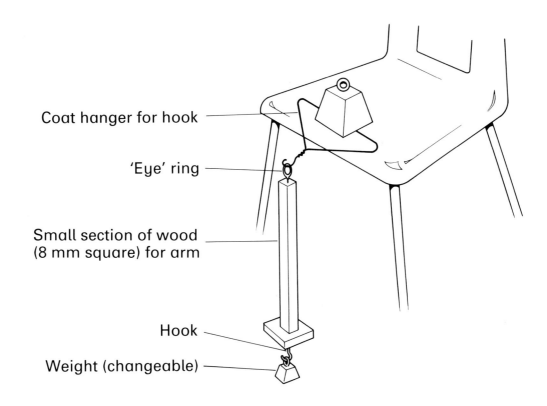

Try to improve the swing, if necessary, by changing the weight, shortening the arm etc.

Changes: Classroom changes

Abacus and counting-board

Abacus

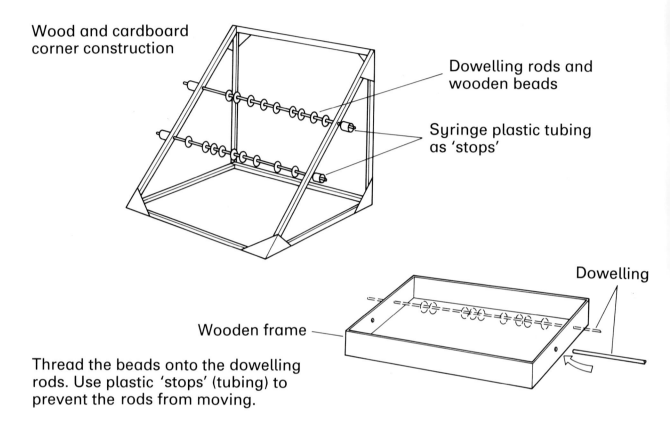

Wood and cardboard corner construction

Dowelling rods and wooden beads

Syringe plastic tubing as 'stops'

Wooden frame

Dowelling

Thread the beads onto the dowelling rods. Use plastic 'stops' (tubing) to prevent the rods from moving.

Counting-board

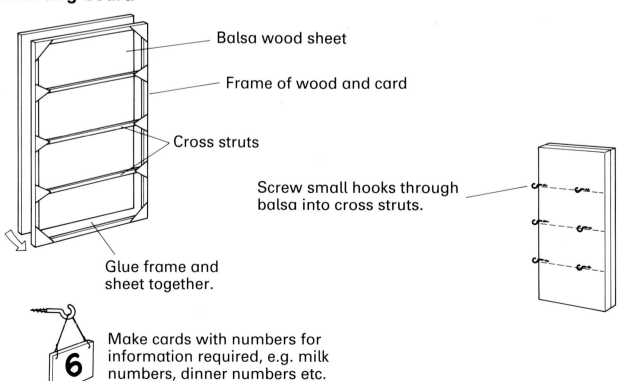

Balsa wood sheet

Frame of wood and card

Cross struts

Screw small hooks through balsa into cross struts.

Glue frame and sheet together.

Make cards with numbers for information required, e.g. milk numbers, dinner numbers etc.

Changes: Classroom changes

Moving windows

Ideas sheet 25

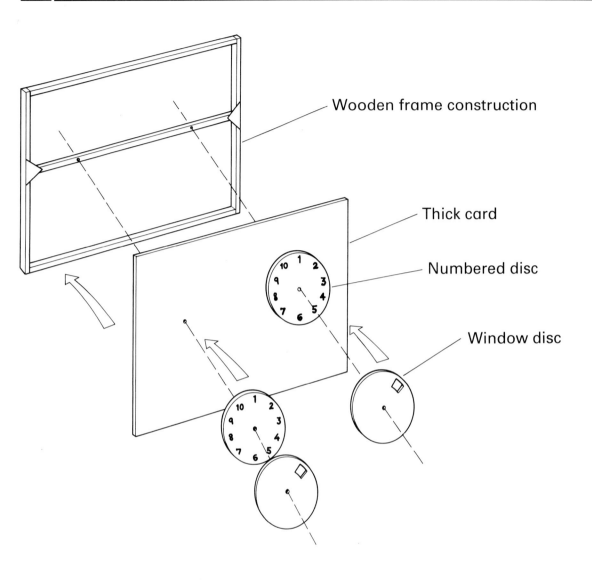

- Wooden frame construction
- Thick card
- Numbered disc
- Window disc

Window disc rotates

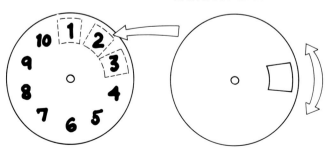

The window disc coincides with the numbered disc to reveal the required digit. Use a paper fastener (split pin) or a short piece of dowel through the centre of the discs.

Changes: Classroom changes

Frame and mould

Ideas sheet 26

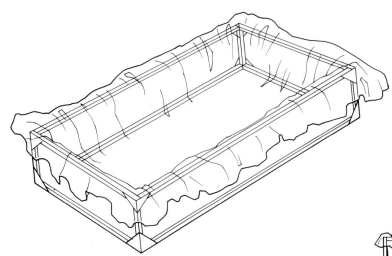

1 Wood and card frame construction lined with a piece of plastic sheeting (an old carrier bag or black sack)

2 Make a clay base and produce an indented pattern.

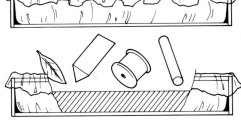

3 Pour plaster onto the clay and let it set.

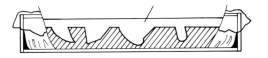

4 Separate the clay and plaster when set.

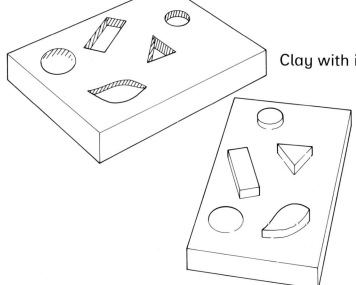

Clay with indented pattern

Plaster with equivalent raised pattern

Changes: Classroom changes

CLASSROOM CHANGES

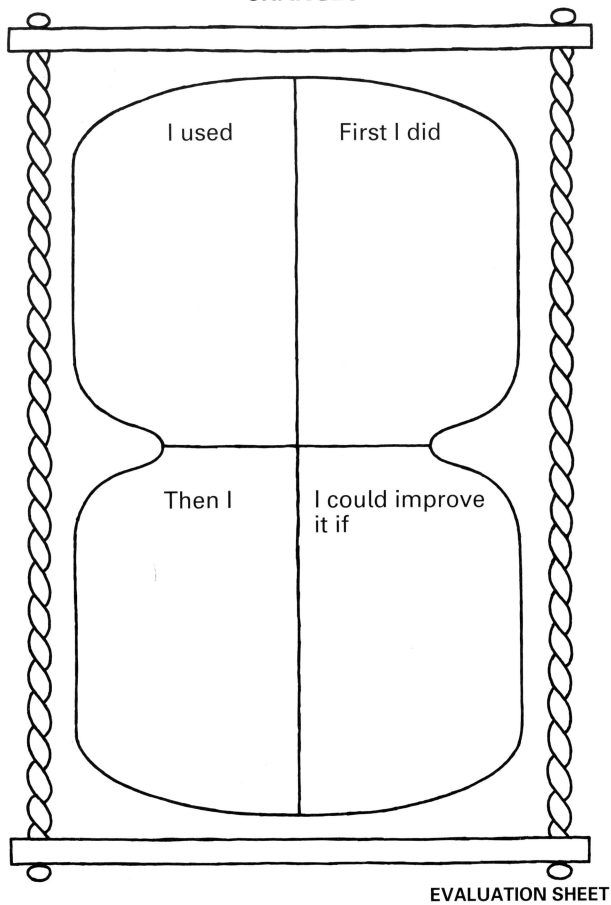

EVALUATION SHEET

Changes: Changes around us

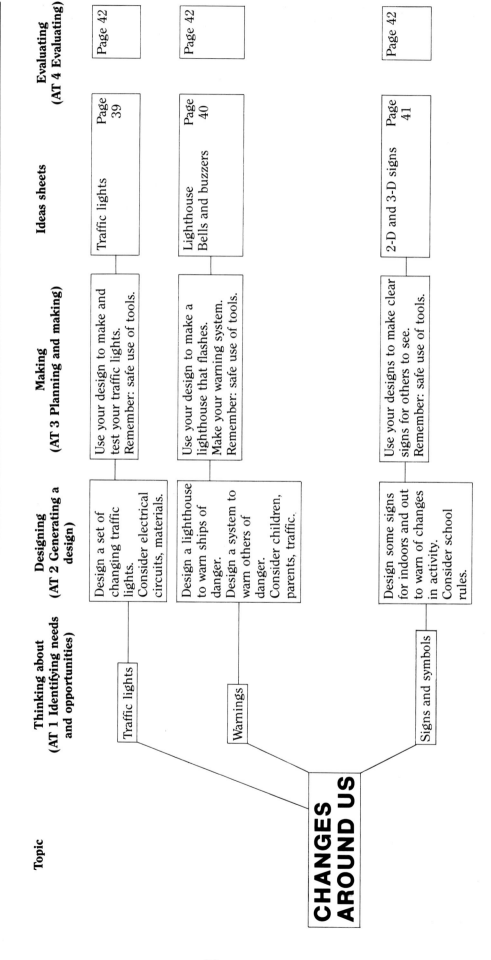

Changes: Changes around us

Traffic lights

Different coloured *cellophane*®

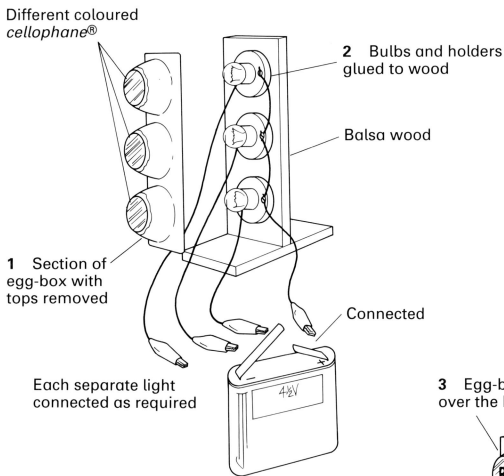

2 Bulbs and holders glued to wood

Balsa wood

1 Section of egg-box with tops removed

Connected

Each separate light connected as required

3 Egg-box fastened over the bulbs

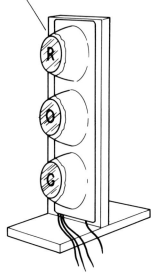

Simple version with two lights only

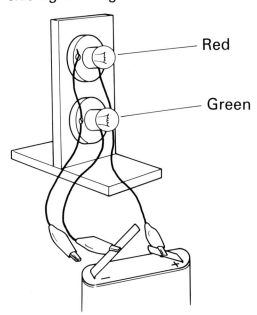

Red

Green

Changes: Changes around us

Lighthouse, bells and buzzers

Lighthouse

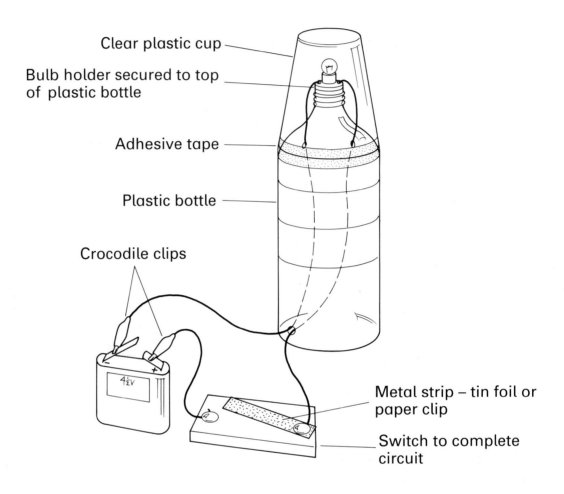

- Clear plastic cup
- Bulb holder secured to top of plastic bottle
- Adhesive tape
- Plastic bottle
- Crocodile clips
- Metal strip – tin foil or paper clip
- Switch to complete circuit

Bells and buzzers

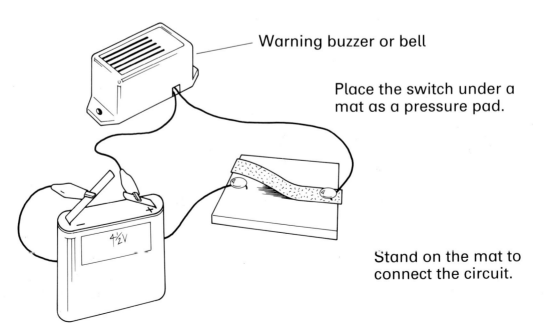

- Warning buzzer or bell
- Place the switch under a mat as a pressure pad.
- Stand on the mat to connect the circuit.

Changes: Changes around us

2-D and 3-D signs

A free-standing warning triangle

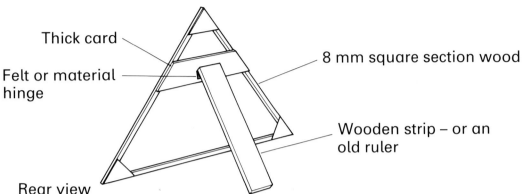

- Thick card
- Felt or material hinge
- 8 mm square section wood
- Wooden strip – or an old ruler

Rear view

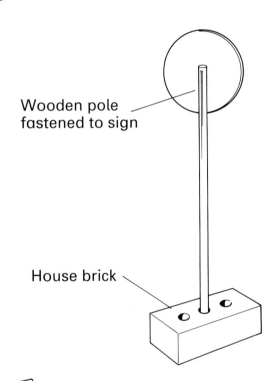

- Wooden pole fastened to sign
- House brick

'A'-frame warning sign

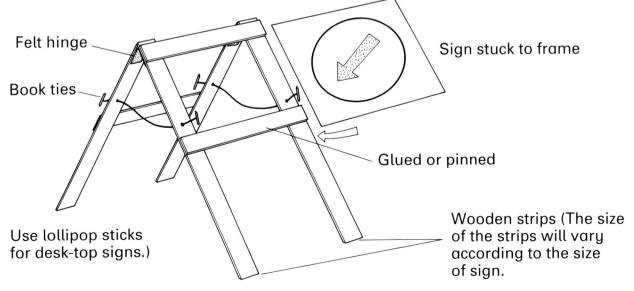

- Felt hinge
- Book ties
- Sign stuck to frame
- Glued or pinned
- Use lollipop sticks for desk-top signs.
- Wooden strips (The size of the strips will vary according to the size of sign.

41

Changes: Changes around us

CHANGES AROUND US

I used

First I did

Then I

I could improve it if

EVALUATION SHEET

Taking care of things: Planning

THEME 3: TAKING CARE OF THINGS

This is a very wide theme that relates well to many activities in infant classrooms. It is built around starting points that are familiar to the children and gives the opportunity to work on a 'life-size' level as well as through models. It would be approached through topics such as Ourselves, My Family, The Home and My School. The two topics developed in the book are **Pets** and **The Playground**.

Science

Living things, conditions for growth, growing plants
Food for life, types of food
Development of egg to chick, baby to adult
Looking after ourselves: healthy bodies, teeth, eyes
Taking care of the world: pollution effects, rubbish, ponds etc.

English

Shopping lists
Letters to friends
Descriptions
Riddles: 'Who is this?'
Recording Science, Maths, Technology work
How I can help
Care of books, book week, sharing books together, writing stories for others to read
Discussion of issues from Science
Handwriting presentation

Mathematics

Measuring, recording plant growth and development: development of egg to chick, bar charts
Dental survey, dental chart, comparison of results, cleaning teeth chart
Time, daily sequence of events in own life, personal routine
Timing activities, skipping, hopping, exercises etc.
Eye chart, distances it can be seen from

Technology

Animal houses, making homes
Storage ideas, making sensible use of space, designing storage at home (e.g. for spoons etc.) and at school
Saving money, money boxes
Taking care of school, fundraising, warning signs to protect children in school, 3-D triangle sign
Shopping aids, making bags, testing strength, model trolleys
Taking care of a baby: safe model rocking cot, rattles and toys, model prams and pushchairs, design and make covers to keep baby dry
Make a tool box
Design a work apron
Welcome to school sign
Make a thimble from junk

Geography

Places in the world needing care, e.g. famine areas, rain forest – identification and discussion

TAKING CARE OF THINGS

RE

Caring for others, relationships, friendship
Families, old and young
Those who care for others, charities, e.g. Red Cross etc.
Taking care of our world, appreciation of its beauty, God's creation
Stories from other religions

Music

Songs about taking care, others in the world

Art

Making cards for families
Tie-dye table-cloth to protect table
Observational work from Science using hand lens, microscope
Pictures of self, portraits of friends, use of mirror

PE

Taking care of our bodies: exercise, swimming, breathing, body awareness

History

Stories about people in the past who have helped others, e.g. Florence Nightingale, Dr. Barnado

43

Taking care of things: Pets

PETS: The design process

Topic	Thinking about (AT 1 Identifying needs and opportunities)	Designing (AT 2 Generating a design)	Making (AT 3 Planning and making)	Ideas sheets	Evaluating (AT 4 Evaluating)
Homes		Design a complete home for a small pet, e.g. a mouse. Consider room to move about, different levels, floors.	Use your design to make a model home for your pet. Remember: safe use of tools.	Model pet's home — Page 45	Page 49
Food and water		Design containers for food and water for your pet. Consider if they are spill-proof. Where should they go?	Use your design to plan and make the containers. Remember: safe use of tools.	Food containers — Page 45	Page 49
Playground		Design and make an exciting adventure playground for a small pet (mouse or hamster). Consider safety, space, size.	Use your design and suitable materials to make the playground. Try it out.	Playground — Page 46	Page 49
Bed		Design a bed for your pet. Consider the size of pet and suitable, safe materials.	Use your design to make a model bed for your pet. Remember: safe use of tools.	Beds for small pets — Page 47 Beds for large pets — Page 48	Page 49

PETS → Homes, Food and water, Playground, Bed

Ideas sheet 30

Model pet's home and pets' food containers

Taking care of things: Pets

Model pet's home

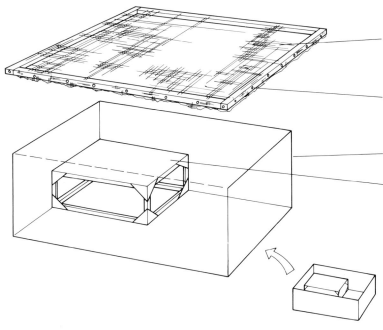

Net curtain stretched over frame

Frame (as lid) with net curtain fastened over

Staples or pins to secure net

Cardboard box without a lid

Timber and cardboard cuboid frame with open sides and wood or cardboard top

Pets' food containers

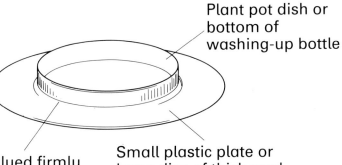

Plant pot dish or bottom of washing-up bottle

Glued firmly

Small plastic plate or large disc of thick card

Pipe cleaner 'hooks'   Holes punched or drilled

Bottom of plastic sauce or shampoo bottle

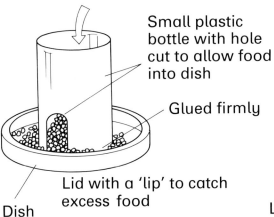

Food in here

Small plastic bottle with hole cut to allow food into dish

Glued firmly

Lid with a 'lip' to catch excess food

Dish

Top of bottle inverted to make spill-proof food container

Lid with a lip

Taking care of things: Pets

Pets' playground

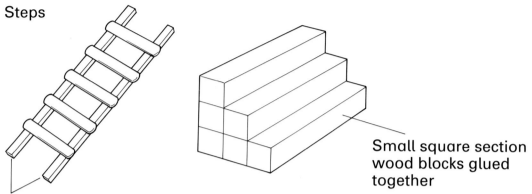

Steps

8 mm square section wood with lollipop sticks or matchsticks for rungs

Small square section wood blocks glued together

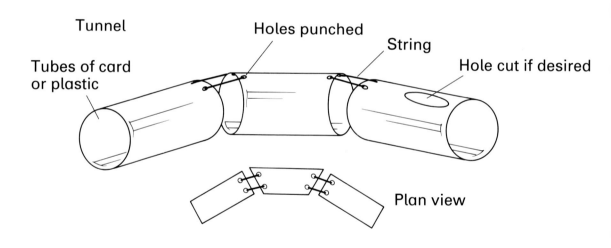

Tunnel

Tubes of card or plastic

Holes punched

String

Hole cut if desired

Plan view

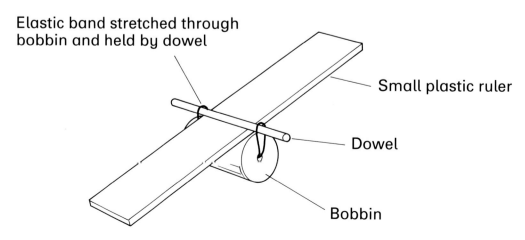

See-saw

Elastic band stretched through bobbin and held by dowel

Small plastic ruler

Dowel

Bobbin

46

Taking care of things: Pets

Small pets' beds

Ideas sheet 32

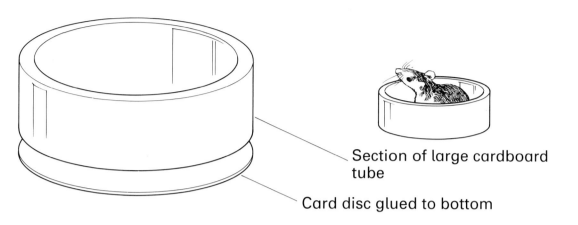

Section of large cardboard tube

Card disc glued to bottom

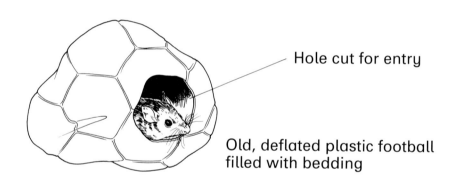

Hole cut for entry

Old, deflated plastic football filled with bedding

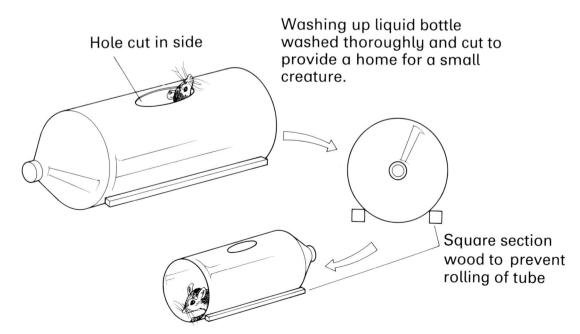

Hole cut in side

Washing up liquid bottle washed thoroughly and cut to provide a home for a small creature.

Square section wood to prevent rolling of tube

47

Taking care of things: Pets

Large pets' beds

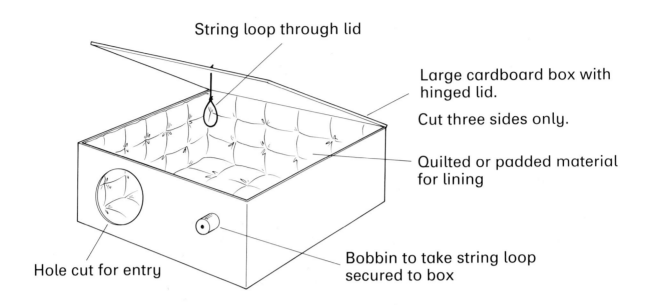

String loop through lid

Large cardboard box with hinged lid.
Cut three sides only.

Quilted or padded material for lining

Hole cut for entry

Bobbin to take string loop secured to box

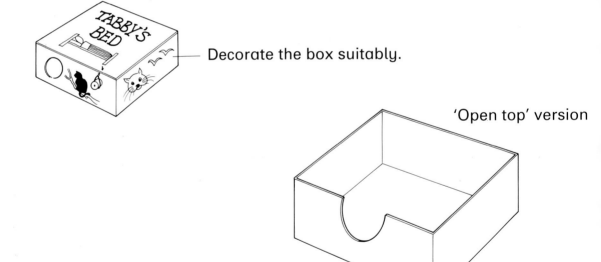

Decorate the box suitably.

'Open top' version

Old washing up bowl decorated and lined with warm, soft material

Paint and PVA glue mixed

Taking care of things: Pets

PETS

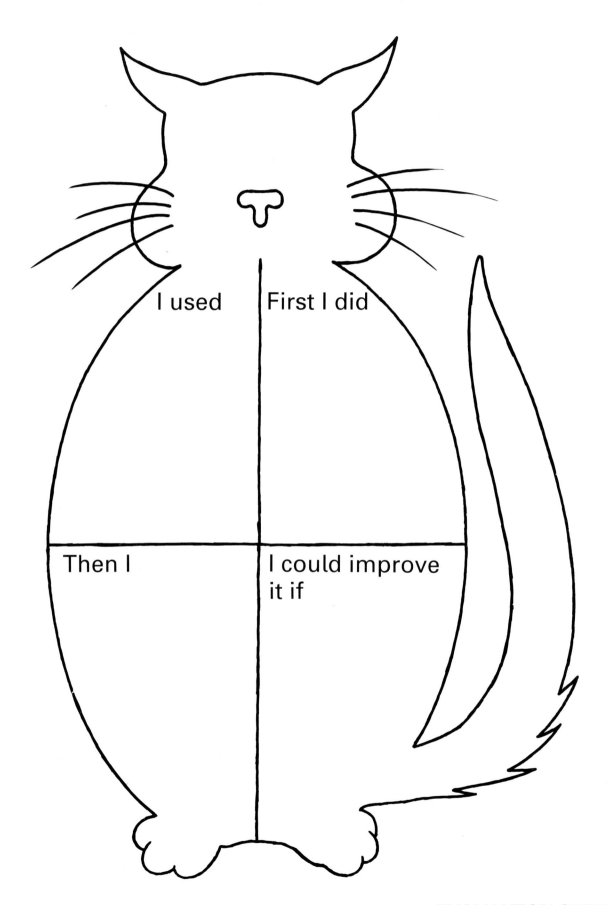

EVALUATION SHEET

Taking care of things: Playground

THE PLAYGROUND: The design process

Topic	Thinking about (AT 1 Identifying needs and opportunities)	Designing (AT 2 Generating a design)	Making (AT 3 Planning and making)	Ideas sheets	Evaluating (AT 4 Evaluating)
Model playground		Design your playground. Consider quiet areas, space, paths, activity areas	Make your model playground. Remember: safe use of tools.	Swings, see-saw, climbing frame — Page 51	Page 56
Playground games and activities		Design a large outdoor game. Consider equipment, safety, rules. Design a wall game. Consider number of players, rules.	Use your design to make your playground activity. Remember: safe use of tools.	Large playground games — Page 52	Page 56
Making the playground look attractive		Design a plant or litter container for your playground. Consider materials, shape, location, safety.	Use your design to make your container. Remember: safe use of tools.	Flower/plant tubs — Page 53 Litter bins — Page 54	Page 56
A nature area		Design a feature to attract wildlife into your playground. Consider birds, butterflies and insects; size, position, safety. Use the design sheet on page 144	Use your design to make your idea. Decide whether it will be life-size or a model. Remember: safe use of tools.	Bird tables — Page 54 Bird feeders — Page 55 Nest box	Page 56

THE PLAYGROUND

50

Taking care of things: Playground

Model playground equipment

Ideas sheet 34

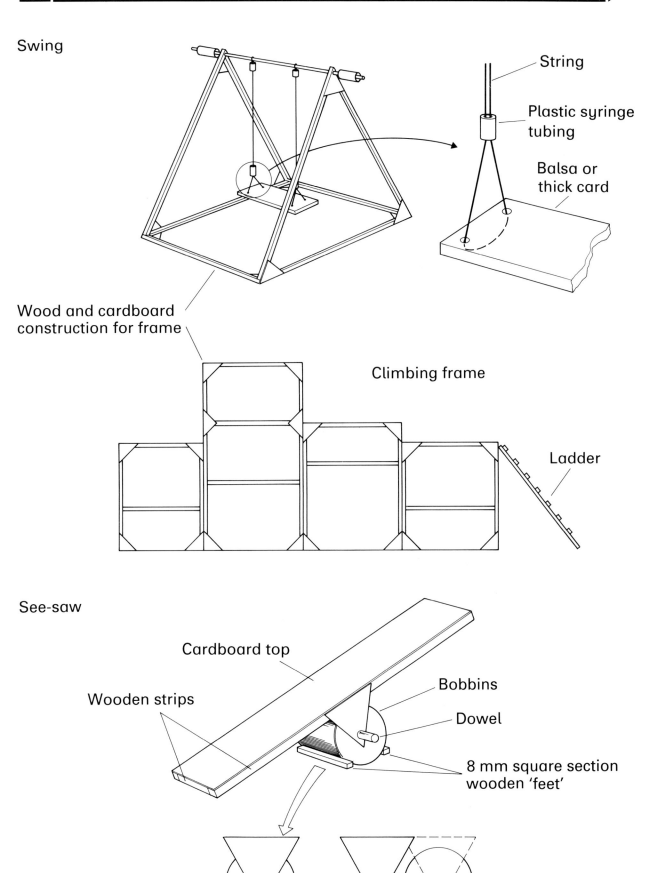

Swing
- String
- Plastic syringe tubing
- Balsa or thick card
- Wood and cardboard construction for frame

Climbing frame
- Ladder

See-saw
- Cardboard top
- Bobbins
- Dowel
- Wooden strips
- 8 mm square section wooden 'feet'

51

Taking care of things: Playground

Large playground games

Skittles game

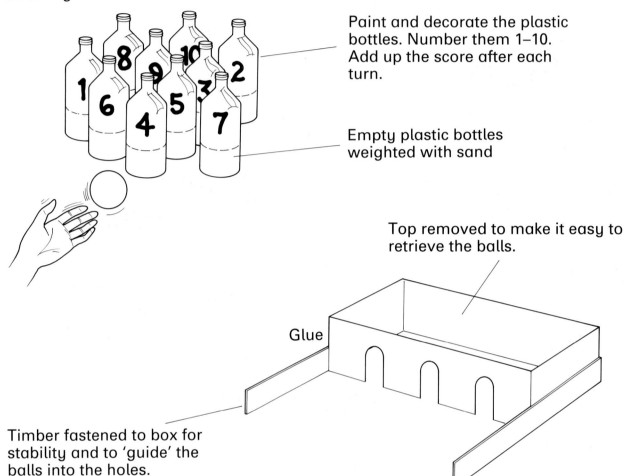

Paint and decorate the plastic bottles. Number them 1–10. Add up the score after each turn.

Empty plastic bottles weighted with sand

Top removed to make it easy to retrieve the balls.

Glue

Timber fastened to box for stability and to 'guide' the balls into the holes.

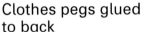

Clothes pegs glued to back

Pegs clipped over bin

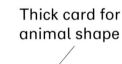

Thick card for animal shape

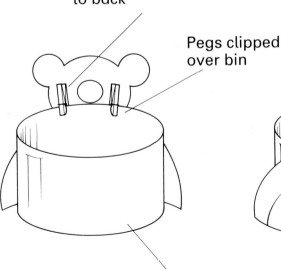

Drum or bin to catch missile

Beanbags or soft ball thrown into the mouth of the animal to 'feed' it.

Taking care of things: Playground

Flower and plant tubs

Ideas sheet 36

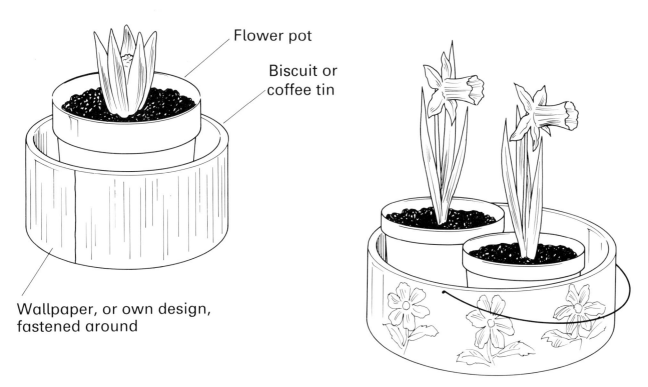

Flower pot

Biscuit or coffee tin

Wallpaper, or own design, fastened around

Use an old powder paint bucket and decorate, perhaps using paint and PVA glue mixed together for a waterproof finish.

Biscuit tin lid

Four strips of wood

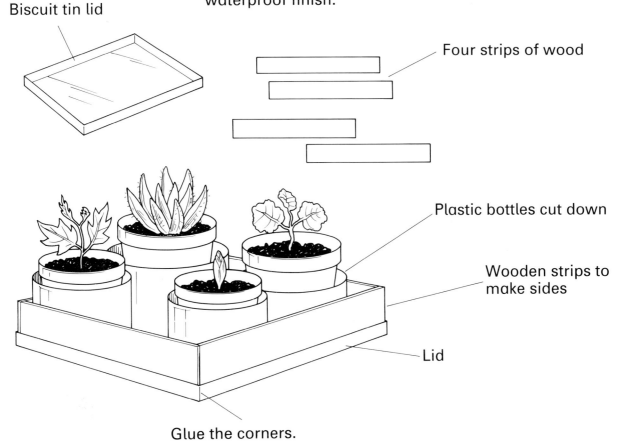

Plastic bottles cut down

Wooden strips to make sides

Lid

Glue the corners.

53

Taking care of things: Playground

Litter bins and bird tables

Litter bins

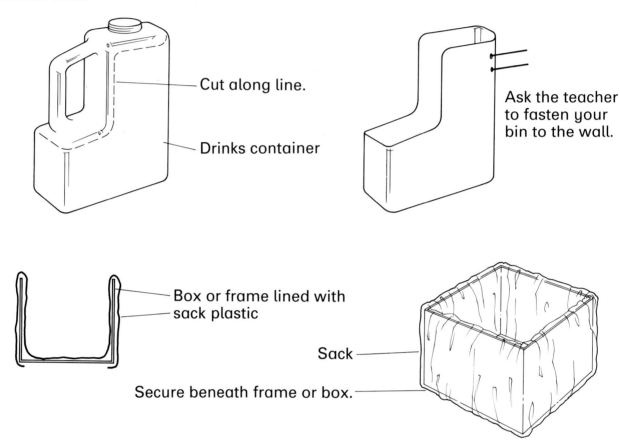

Cut along line.

Drinks container

Ask the teacher to fasten your bin to the wall.

Box or frame lined with sack plastic

Sack

Secure beneath frame or box.

Model bird table

Tabs folded for glue

Cardboard

Card tubes

'L' shaped brackets for support

Card pieces

Large tube in container

Hanging bird table

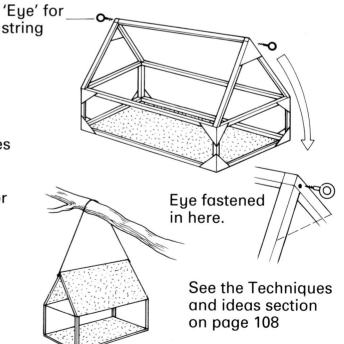

'Eye' for string

Eye fastened in here.

See the Techniques and ideas section on page 108

54

Taking care of things: Playground

Bird feeders and nest box

Bird feeders

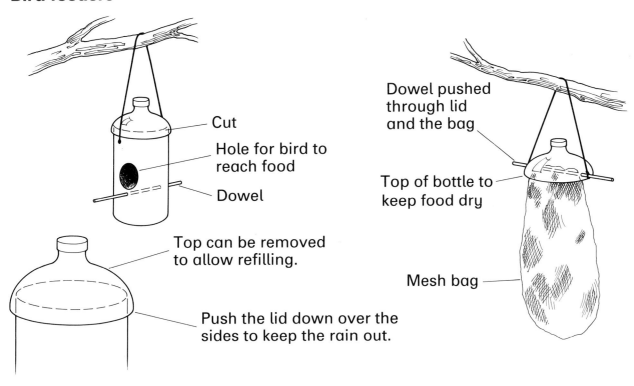

Nest box

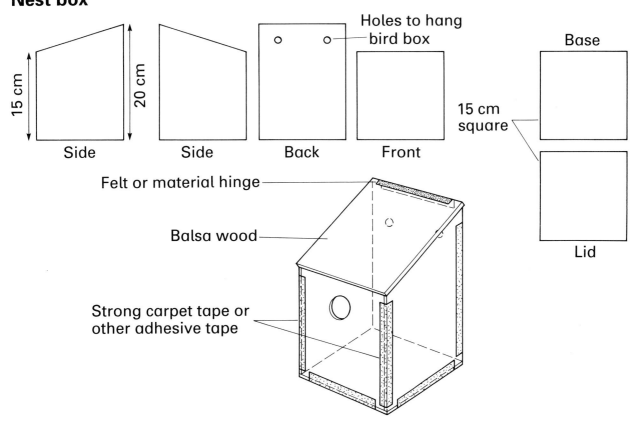

Taking care of things: Playground

THE PLAYGROUND

I used

First I did

Then I

I could improve it if

EVALUATION SHEET

THEME 4: STRUCTURES

This theme is perhaps the one that is most readily associated with Technology. It would easily present a term's work and could develop a wide range of mathematical skills and knowledge. It is likely that the theme will involve children making visits to nearby places. **Houses** and **The Building Site** are the two areas developed in detail within the theme, but other routes into the theme could be topics on Transport, Our Town or My Home.

Technology

Building and testing model structures using a range of materials: houses, furniture, garage
Scaffolding
Bridges
Wood, newspaper, glue and strengthening techniques
Keeping safe on building sites, making protective clothing
The playground, structures, climbing frame, design and layout

Science

Animal structures (bees, wasps, ants)
Shells, spirals
Natural structures: seed heads, cases, flower heads
Flying structures: kites, parachutes etc.
Internal structures, skeletons (of humans and animals)
Fair tests of structures
Materials; qualities, suitability for tasks
Homes, circuits

English

Discussion about observations
Descriptions of objects
Recording experiments, science activities
Poems
Stories
Talking/ vocabulary in structured play situations: building site, house, playground
Using reference materials
Charts

Mathematics

3-D shapes
Tessellation: 2-D, 3-D
Money and number work from visits
Measurement, estimation
Select materials, measures
Data collection on houses
Right angles, corners

Geography

Visits, routes to building site
Look at famous structures and locate, e.g. Blackpool Tower, Leaning tower of Pisa, Big Ben

RE

Family tree, family ties
Co-operation games, turn taking
Caring for the community, handicapped people

Music

Structure of music: notes, simple recording using tonic so-fa scale
Sound patterns
Counting, clapping rhythm

Art

Observational work using microscope of natural structures
Making kites, using fabrics, decorating
Designing wallpaper and curtains using dye, fabric, crayons and printing
Paper sculpture
Clay work for making structures
3-D skeletons

PE

Using apparatus structures
Making structures with own bodies
Cooperating with others

History

Family tree, relations

Structures: Houses

HOUSES: The design process

Topic	Thinking about (AT 1 Identifying needs and opportunities)	Designing (AT 2 Generating a design)	Making (AT 3 Planning and making)	Ideas sheets	Evaluating (AT 4 Evaluating)
HOUSES → The building	The building	Design the house you are going to build. Consider framework, doors, roof, windows.	Use your design to make your house with suitable materials. Remember: safe use of tools.	Roofs — Page 59	Page 67
HOUSES → Bedroom	Bedroom	Design a new bedroom for yourself. Design new wallpaper for your room.	Use your design to make a model of your bedroom. Use your design to make your own wallpaper by printing or painting. Remember: safe use of tools.	Planning bedroom design — Page 60; Grid sheets for wallpaper design — Page 61, 62	Page 67
HOUSES → Bunk bed	Bunk bed	Design a bunk bed to fit in your model house. Design a toy box for a favourite toy.	Use your design to make your model bunk bed. Use your design to make your toy box.	Bunk beds — Page 63; Toy box and containers — Page 64	Page 67
HOUSES → Garage	Garage	Design a garage for your car. Consider how the door will open, space, windows, size of car.	Use your design to make your model garage. Remember: safe use of tools.	Garages — Page 65; Openings, Hinges — Page 66	Page 67

58

Roofs

Structures: Houses

Ideas sheet 39

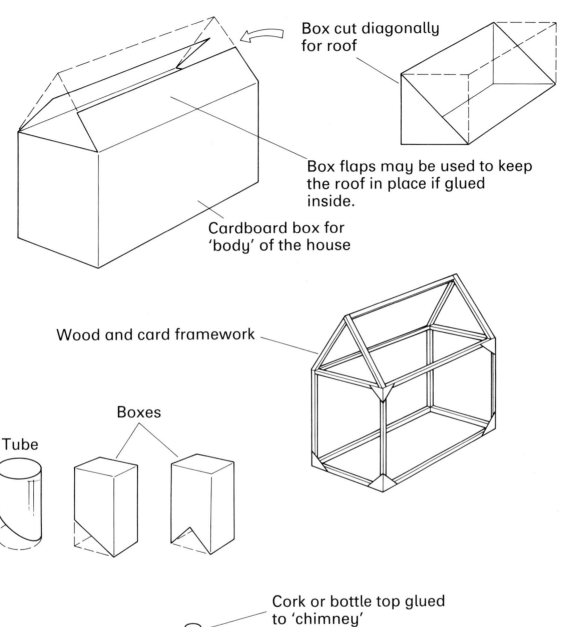

Box cut diagonally for roof

Box flaps may be used to keep the roof in place if glued inside.

Cardboard box for 'body' of the house

Wood and card framework

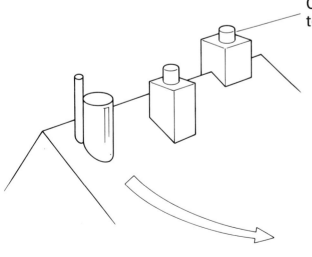

Tube

Boxes

Cork or bottle top glued to 'chimney'

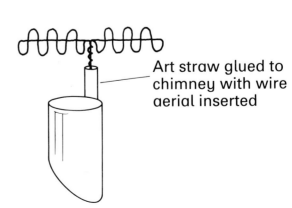

Art straw glued to chimney with wire aerial inserted

59

Structures: Houses

Planning bedroom

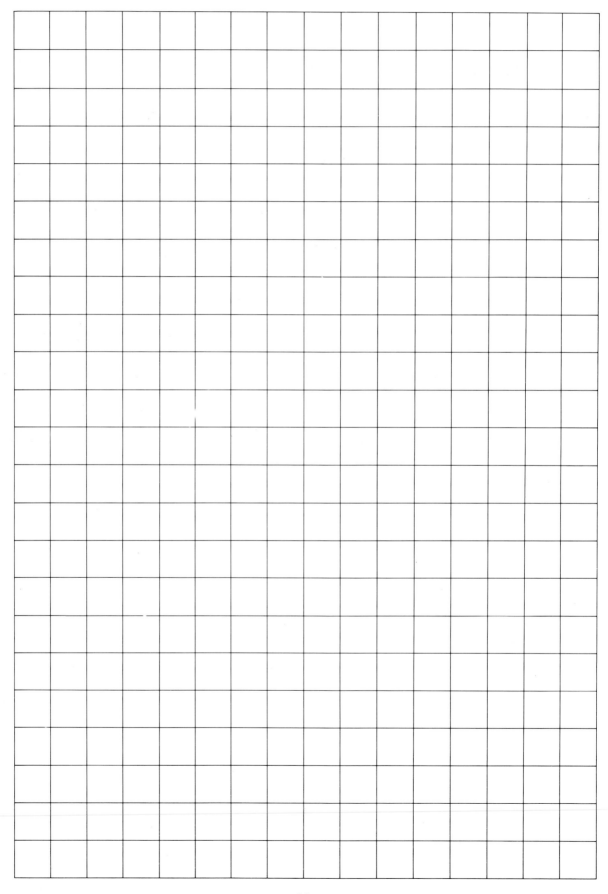

60

Structures: Houses

Wallpaper design 1

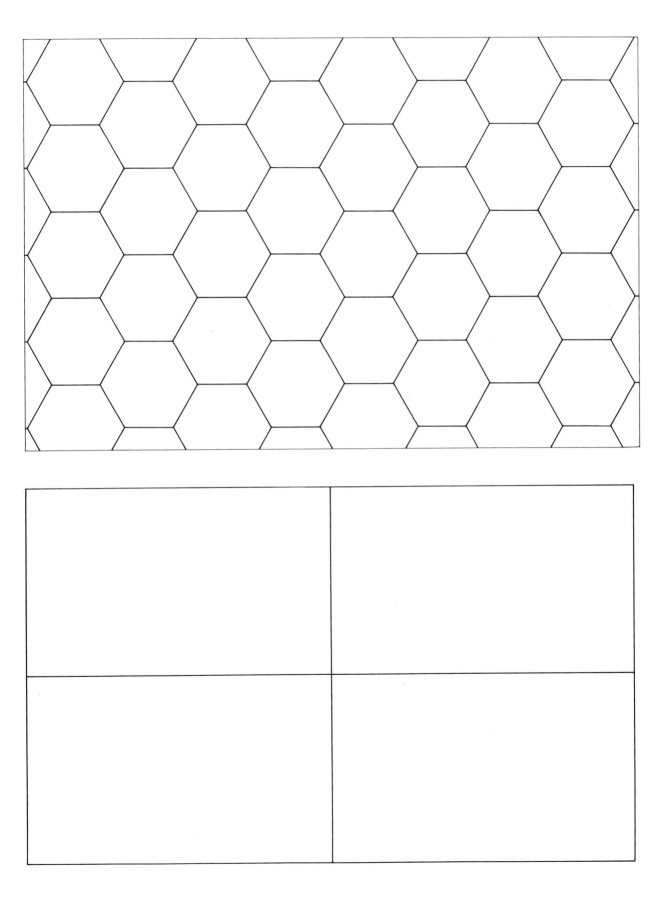

Structures: Houses

Ideas sheet 42

Wallpaper design 2

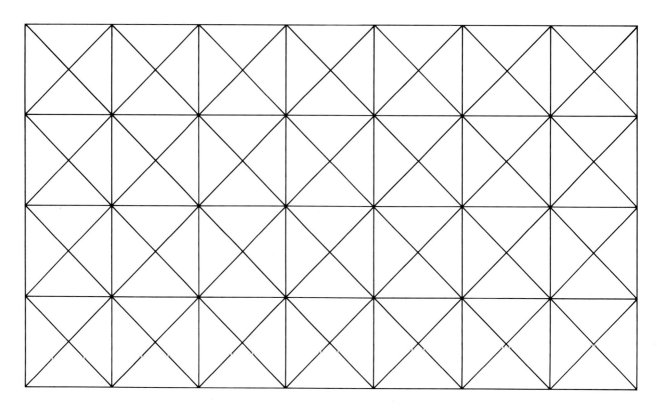

Wallpaper design 2

Structures: Houses

Bunk beds

Ideas sheet 43

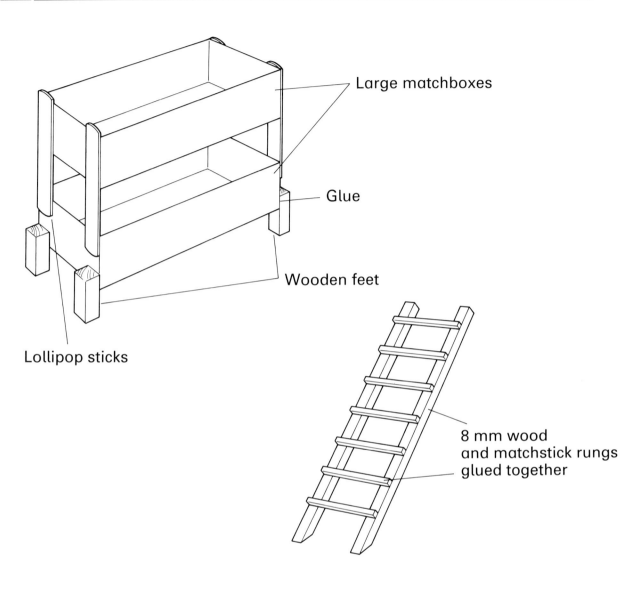

Large matchboxes

Glue

Wooden feet

Lollipop sticks

8 mm wood and matchstick rungs glued together

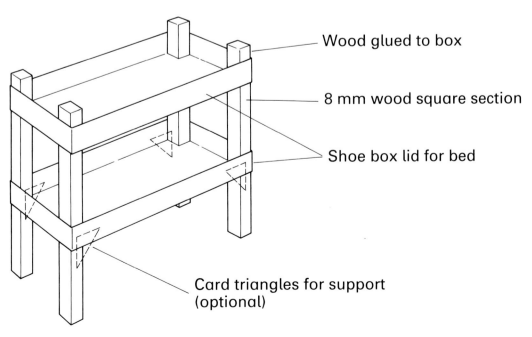

Wood glued to box

8 mm wood square section

Shoe box lid for bed

Card triangles for support (optional)

63

Structures: Houses

Toy box and containers

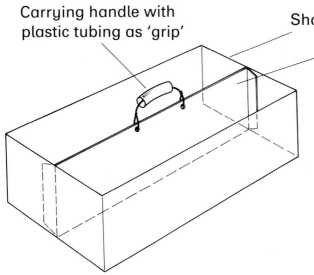

Carrying handle with plastic tubing as 'grip'

Shoe box or similar

Centre piece of thick card glued to end of box

Decorate with paint, felt, crayons etc.

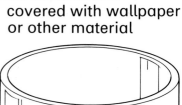

Large empty coffee tin cleaned and covered with wallpaper or other material

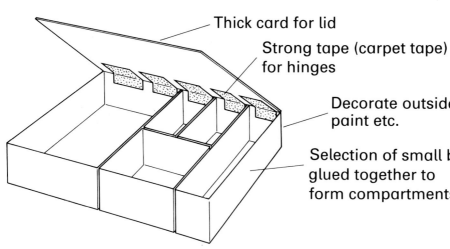

Thick card for lid

Strong tape (carpet tape) for hinges

Decorate outside with wallpaper, fabric paint etc.

Selection of small boxes glued together to form compartments

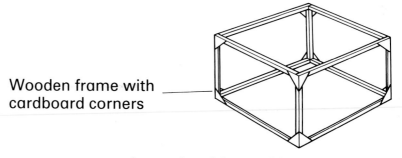

Wooden frame with cardboard corners

Cover the sides and base with thick card and decorate with paint or felt

Structures: Houses

Garages

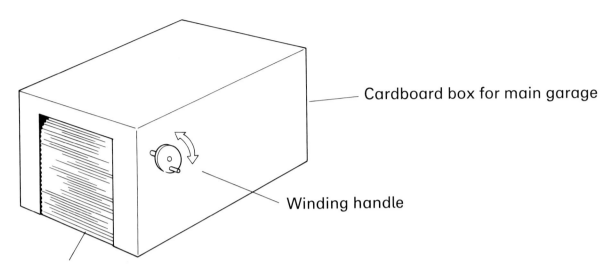

Cardboard box for main garage

Winding handle

Corrugated card for door glued at top to winding mechanism

Detail of winding mechanism

Cotton reels and dowel glued in centre hole

Plastic tubing as 'stop'

Disc and handle

Dowel

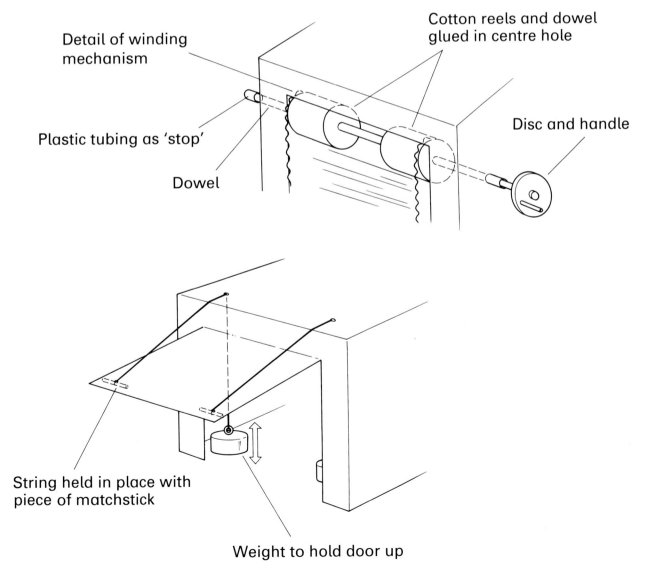

String held in place with piece of matchstick

Weight to hold door up

Structures: Houses

Openings and hinges

Openings

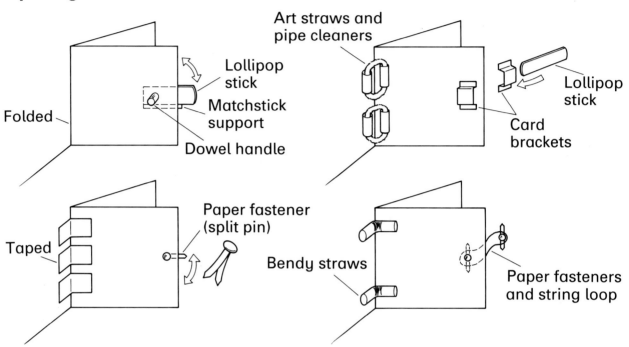

Hinges

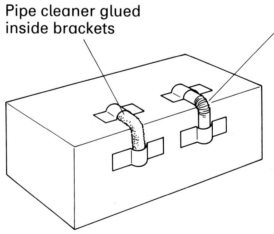

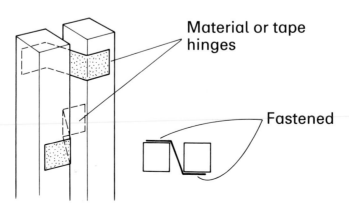

HOUSES

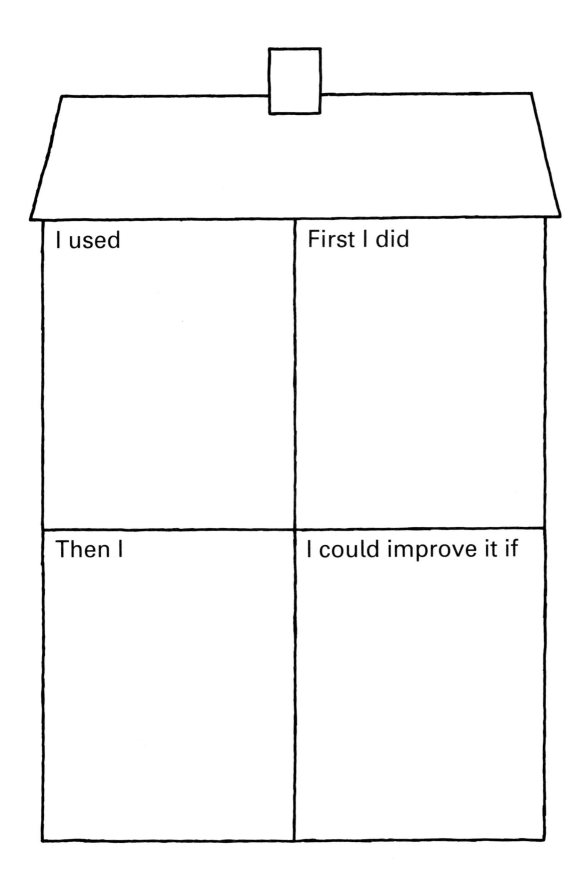

EVALUATION SHEET

Structures: Building site

THE BUILDING SITE: The design process

Topic	Thinking about (AT 1 Identifying needs and opportunities)	Designing (AT 2 Generating a design)	Making (AT 3 Planning and making)	Ideas sheets	Evaluating (AT 4 Evaluating)
THE BUILDING SITE	People who work on the site	Design ways of keeping people safe. Consider heads, feet, hands.	Make your design to keep people safe. Remember: safe use of tools.	Hard hat / Safety clothes — Page 69	Page 73
	Safety	Design a variety of ways to keep bricks, pipes, wood etc. safe and tidy. Consider space, traffic.	Use your design to make something to store materials safely and tidily. Remember: safe use of tools.	Models storage systems — Page 70	Page 73
	Vehicles and machines	Design a vehicle or machine for a building site, e.g. tip-up lorry, bulldozer, road-roller.	Use your design to make your moving vehicle or machine. Remember: safe use of tools.	Bulldozer and road roller — Page 71	Page 73
	Scaffolding	Design some scaffolding which will stand firmly and hold a heavy weight. Consider shapes.	Use your design to make scaffolding. Consider a wide variety of materials. Test your scaffolding. Remember: safe use of tools.	Joining ideas / Scaffolding — Page 72	Page 73

68

Structures: Building site

Hard hat and safety clothes

Hard hat

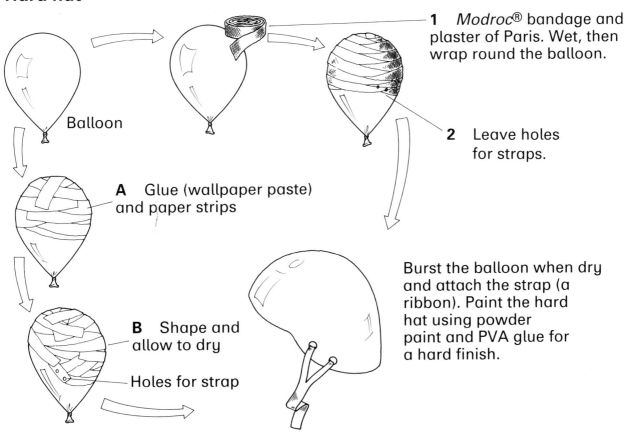

Safety clothes

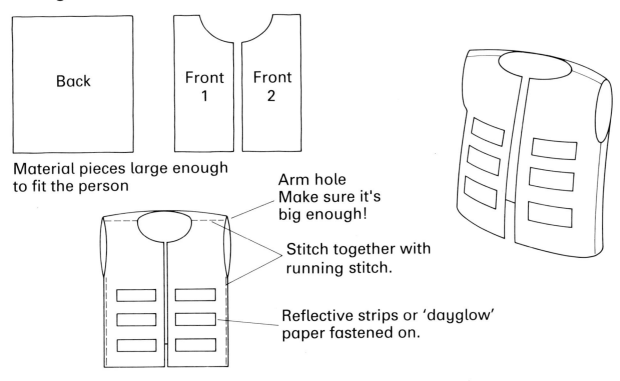

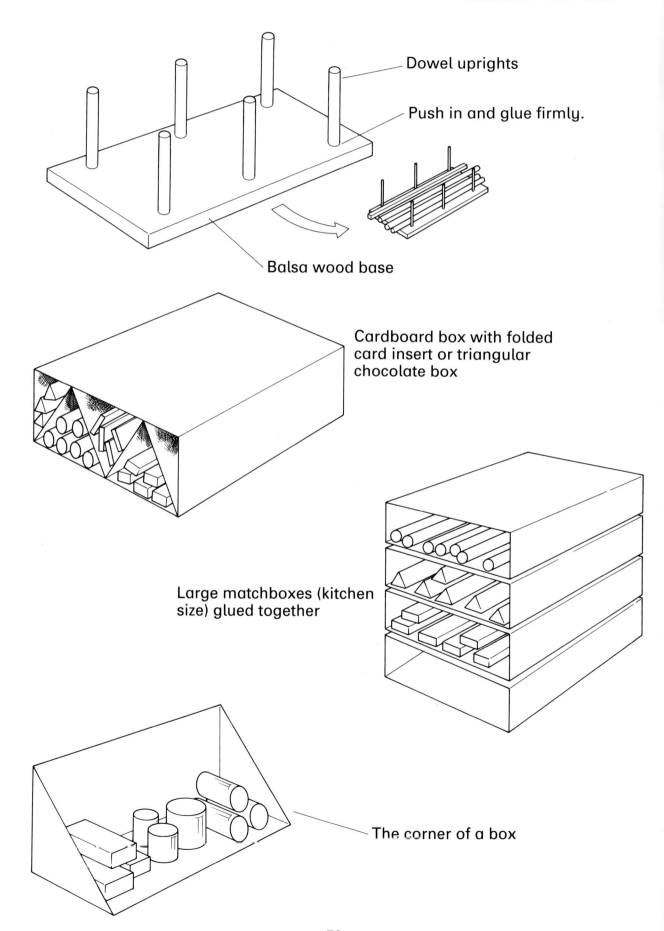

Structures: Building site

Bulldozer and road roller

Bulldozer

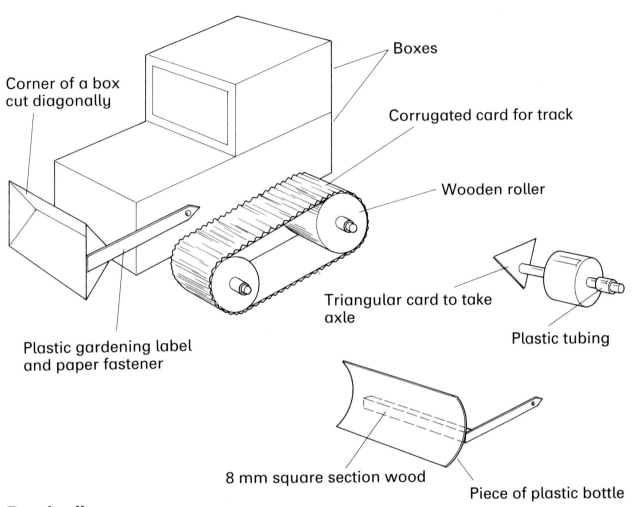

- Boxes
- Corner of a box cut diagonally
- Corrugated card for track
- Wooden roller
- Triangular card to take axle
- Plastic tubing
- Plastic gardening label and paper fastener
- 8 mm square section wood
- Piece of plastic bottle

Road roller

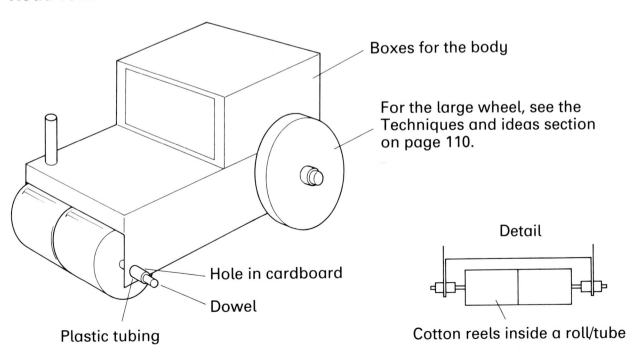

- Boxes for the body
- For the large wheel, see the Techniques and ideas section on page 110.
- Hole in cardboard
- Dowel
- Plastic tubing

Detail

Cotton reels inside a roll/tube

Structures: Building site

Scaffolding

Newspaper 'rolls'

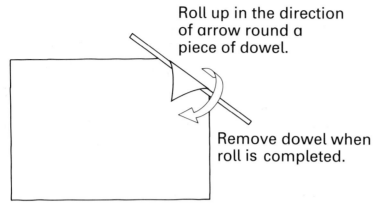

Roll up in the direction of arrow round a piece of dowel.

Remove dowel when roll is completed.

Use masking tape to join the rolls.

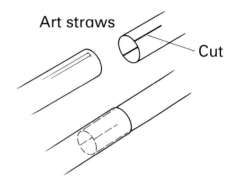

Art straws

Cut

Push together and glue. Allow to dry.

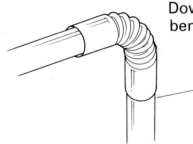

Dowelling and bendy straws

Glue dowelling to straw.

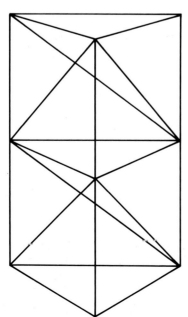

Suggested structure for straws/newspaper

Wood and card construction

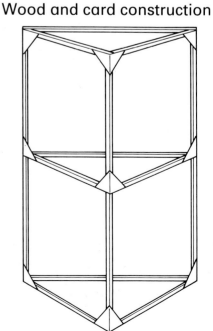

Structures: Building site

THE BUILDING SITE

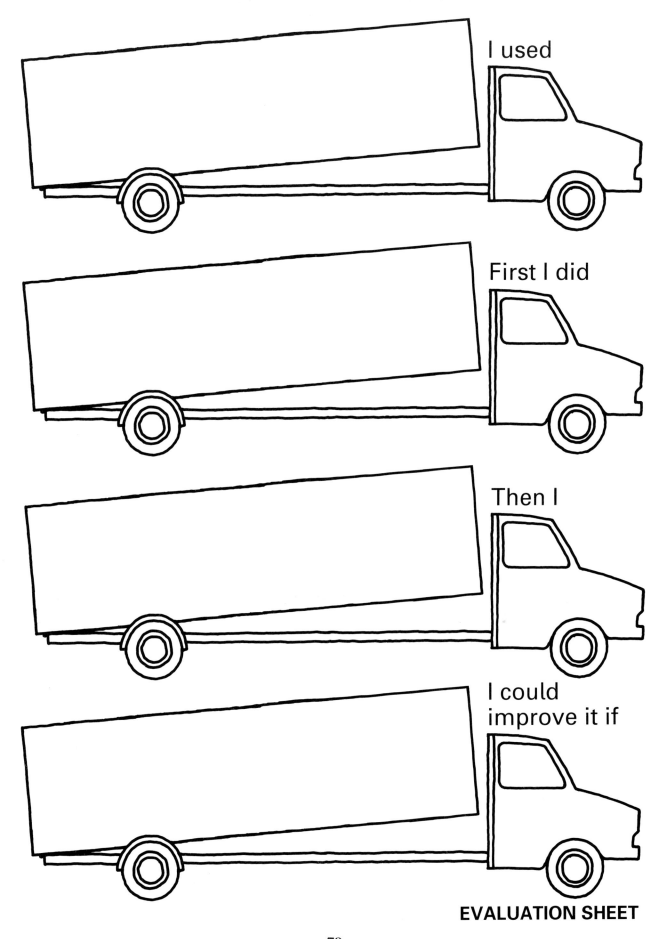

I used

First I did

Then I

I could improve it if

EVALUATION SHEET

Out and about: Planning

THEME 5: OUT AND ABOUT

This theme will involve the children using their own local environment and their own experiences of local events and places. **Direction Games** has been developed as a topic as it has strong cross-curricular links with Mathematics. **Holidays** presents the children with opportunities to use materials other than wood and junk, and to work at a 'life-size' level. Teachers could also approach this theme from topics on Clothing, The Circus and Shops and Shopping.

Science

Exploration of immediate locality
Sort and classify insects, plants, water creatures and their habitats
Collections, microscope use
Animal journeys, migration
Air, flying, aeroplanes
Magnets
Circuits, electricity
Pollution, traffic
Rubbish, litter, decay

Mathematics

Shapes in the environment
Direction games
Grids and maps
Language of direction (horizontal, vertical)
Timing journeys, journey problems, simple timetables
Shoe sizes
Census and traffic counts
Money work, shopping

English

Discussions, observations on visits out, signs, sights, what do we take on journeys?
Lists
Letters
Adventure journeys
Reference work about the environment
Descriptions
Estate Agent's shop: play situations
Café – menus
Tape recordings
Sound poems
Recording results of science observations

Technology

Journey to school: keeping safe (armbands, helmets, designs)
Direction games to make
Flying planes, gliders etc.
Model boats
Holiday journeys: caravans, bags, sun-hats
Fairground models: swings, roundabouts, helter-skelters
Maps and models of locations, roadways
Shops, the role of shopping

Geography

Holidays: where do we go?
Simple maps, directions, the four compass points
Travel
Sending letters to places

OUT AND ABOUT

RE

Visit local church, mosque etc.
Co-operation, team work, games

Music

Rhythms of the street: feet, noises, horns etc.
Setting poems about the street to percussion

Art

Printing: tickets, footprints, wheels
Observational drawings of plants and insects with a range of media
Fabric work, sewing, collage
Houses: colours, brick patterns, 3-D clay work, tiles

PE

Directions
Levels
Fast/slow

History

Old buildings
Local history, events, people

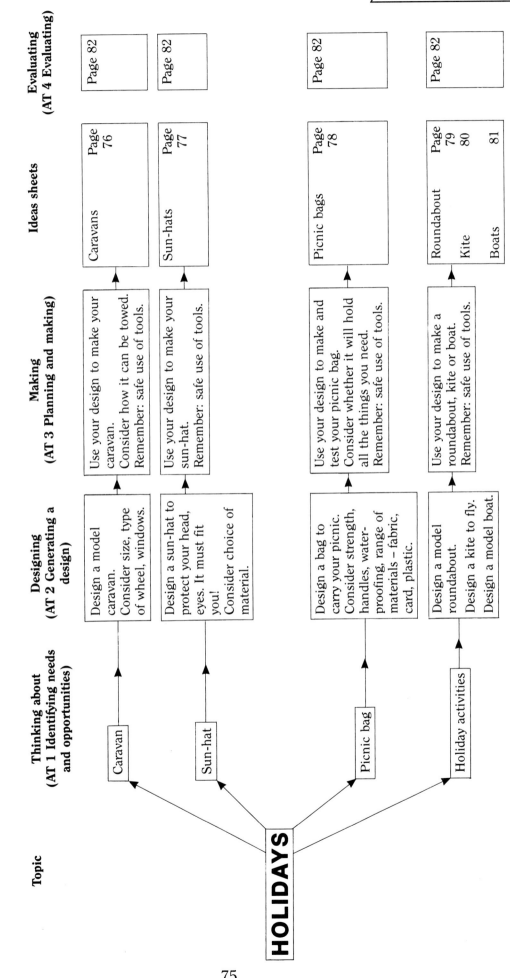

Out and about: Holidays

Ideas sheet 51

Caravans

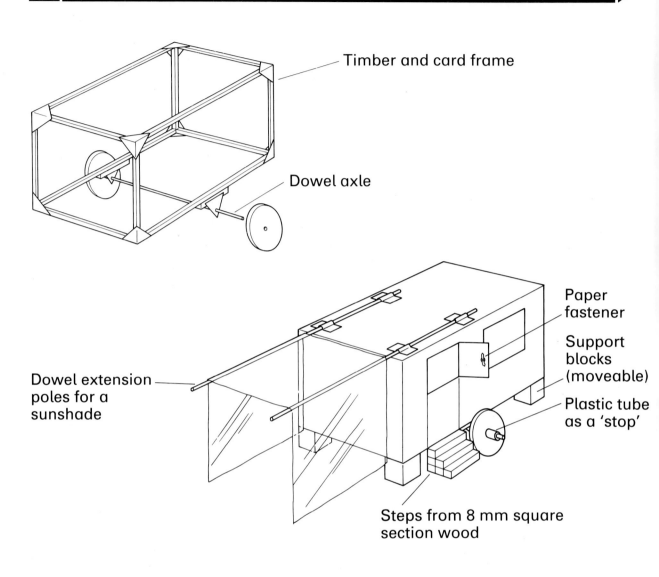

Timber and card frame

Dowel axle

Dowel extension poles for a sunshade

Paper fastener

Support blocks (moveable)

Plastic tube as a 'stop'

Steps from 8 mm square section wood

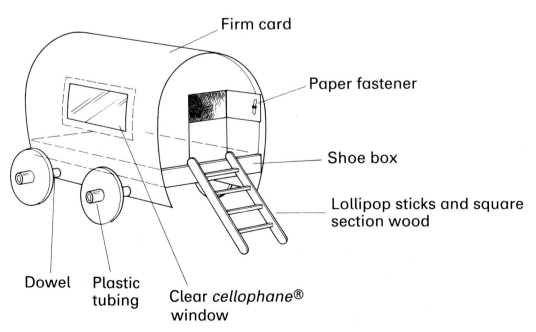

Firm card

Paper fastener

Shoe box

Lollipop sticks and square section wood

Dowel   Plastic tubing

Clear *cellophane*® window

76

Out and about: Holidays

Sun-hats

Ideas sheet 52

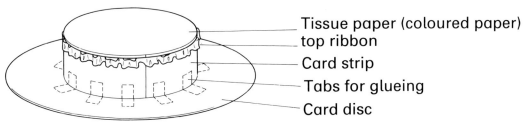

Card circle

B A

Cut

Cut and overlap edges **A** and **B** to form a shallow cone.

Decorate with ribbons of tissue.

Matchstick Edge of hat String to hold hat on head

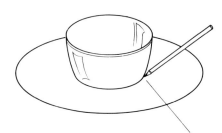

Tissue paper (coloured paper)
top ribbon
Card strip
Tabs for glueing
Card disc

Draw round the base of a margarine tub. Cut out the circle.

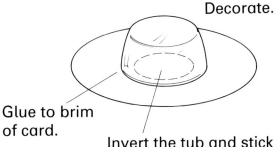

Decorate.

Glue to brim of card.

Invert the tub and stick over hole.

1 Card strip long enough to fit round child's head

2 Card peak and strip

Fold line

3 Fit together to make a visor.

4 Glue together and decorate.

77

Out and about: Holidays

Ideas sheet 53

Picnic bags

1 Holes for the handle

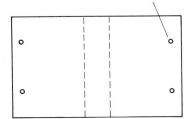

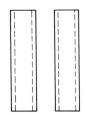

2 Wide strips of paper and card for the ends of the bag

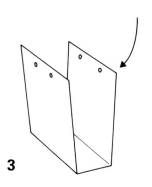

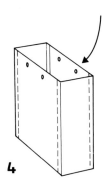

3

4

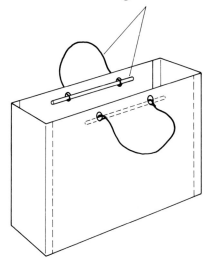

5 To fit the handle use string and dowel

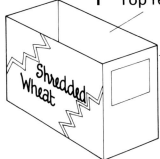

1 Top removed

Large cereal box

If possible unfasten the edges and turn the box inside out.

The children are then painting onto a clean 'matt' surface.

3 Fasten on the handles with string and dowel.

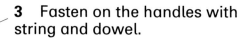

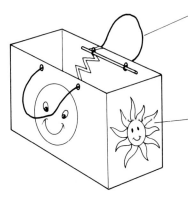

2 Decorate the box brightly.

78

Out and about: Holidays

Roundabout

Ideas sheet 54

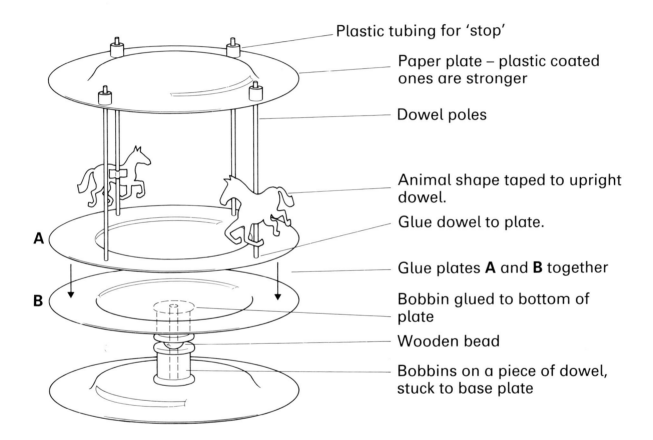

- Plastic tubing for 'stop'
- Paper plate – plastic coated ones are stronger
- Dowel poles
- Animal shape taped to upright dowel.
- Glue dowel to plate.
- Glue plates **A** and **B** together
- Bobbin glued to bottom of plate
- Wooden bead
- Bobbins on a piece of dowel, stuck to base plate

79

Out and about: Holidays

Kite

Ideas sheet 55

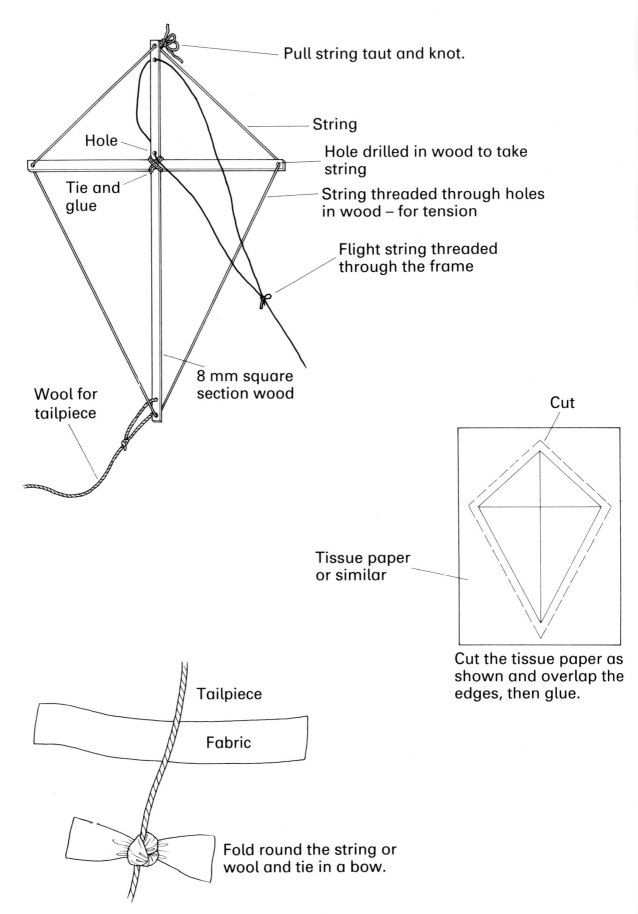

Out and about: Holidays

Boats

Ideas sheet 56

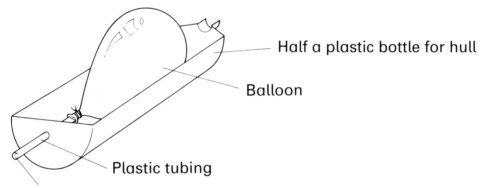

Plastic corrugated sheet

Dowel pushed through plastic

Glue the dowel first. Allow to dry.

Elastic band stretched round the neck

Direction of turn of paddle

Half a plastic washing-up bottle

Half a plastic bottle for hull

Balloon

Plastic tubing

Inflate the balloon by blowing into the tubing.

Wood block and side pieces

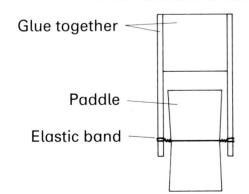

Glue together

Paddle

Elastic band

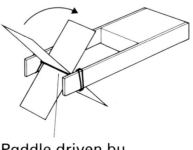

Paddle driven by elastic band

81

Out and about: Holidays

HOLIDAYS

I used

First I did

Then I

I could improve it if

EVALUATION SHEET

Out and about: Direction games

DIRECTION GAMES: The design process

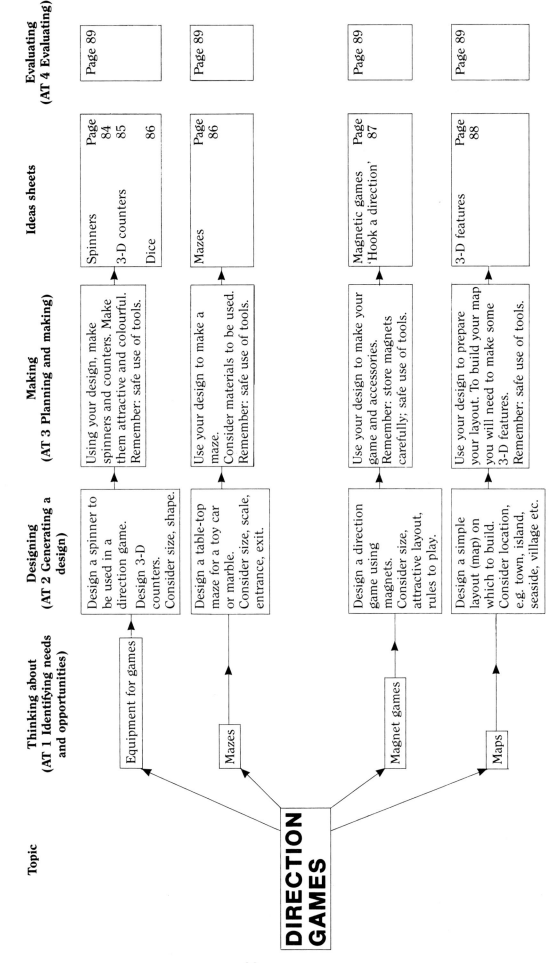

Out and about: Direction games

Spinners

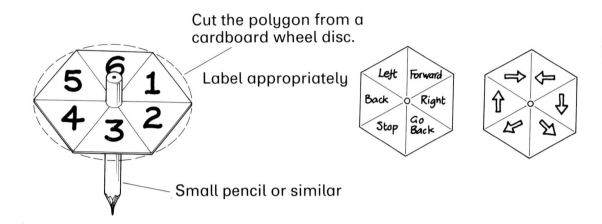

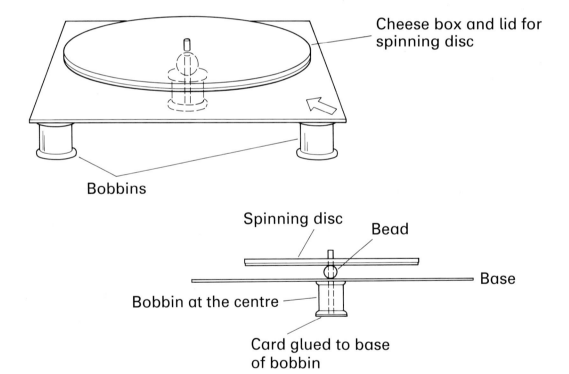

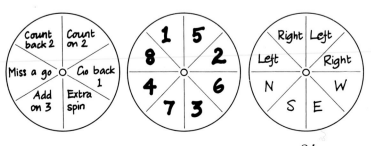

Suggestions for spinning disc

Out and about: Direction games

Ideas sheet 58

3-D counters

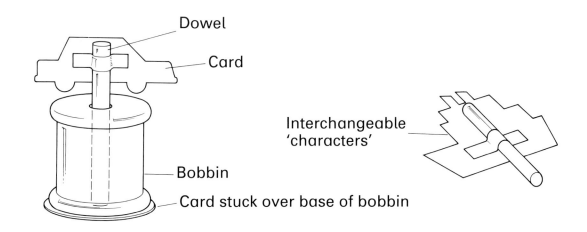

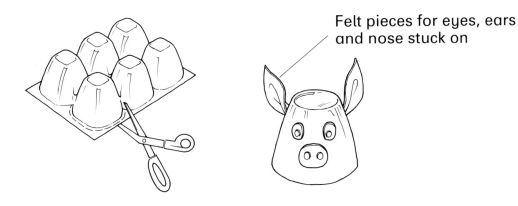

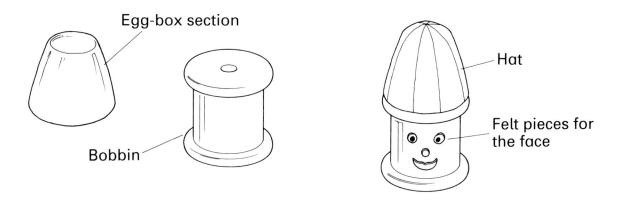

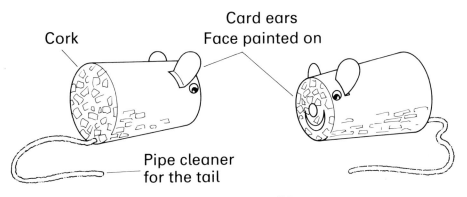

Out and about: Direction games

Dice and mazes

Dice

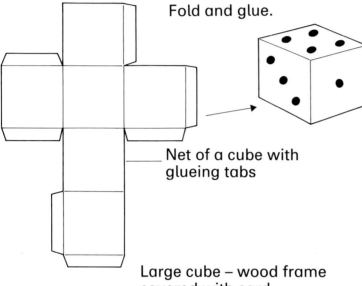

Fold and glue.

Net of a cube with glueing tabs

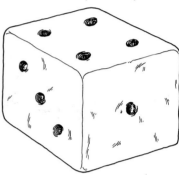

Clay cube with numbers pushed in with a pencil point

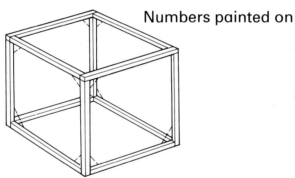

Large cube – wood frame covered with card
Numbers painted on

Deep foam rubber (very soft)

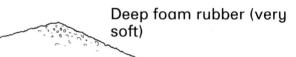

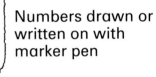

Numbers drawn or written on with marker pen

Mazes

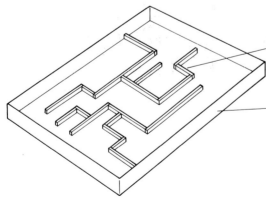

8 mm wood pieces stuck to base

Cardboard base with sides, e.g. cardboard box lid

Marble maze

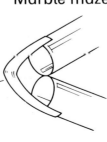
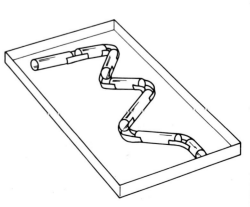

Card tubes glued to base board and connected by strips to prevent the marble from spilling out

Out and about: Direction games

Magnetic games and 'Hook a direction'

Magnetic games

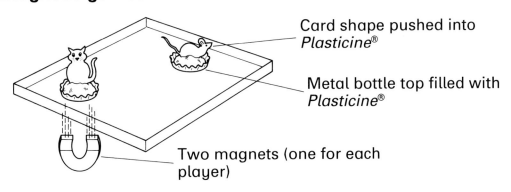

Card shape pushed into *Plasticine*®

Metal bottle top filled with *Plasticine*®

Two magnets (one for each player)

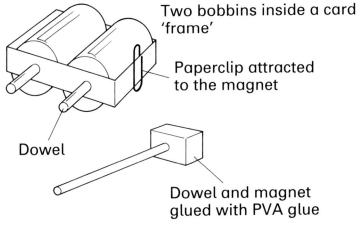

Simple vehicle

Two bobbins inside a card 'frame'

Paperclip attracted to the magnet

Dowel

Dowel and magnet glued with PVA glue

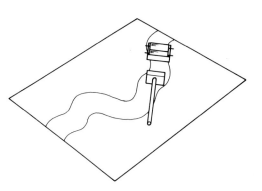

'Hook a direction'

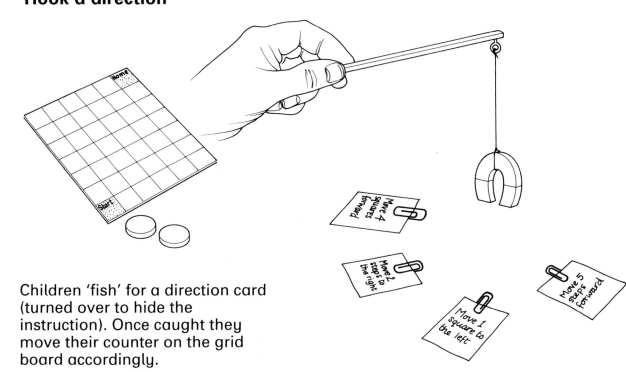

Children 'fish' for a direction card (turned over to hide the instruction). Once caught they move their counter on the grid board accordingly.

Out and about: Direction games

Ideas sheet 61

3-D features

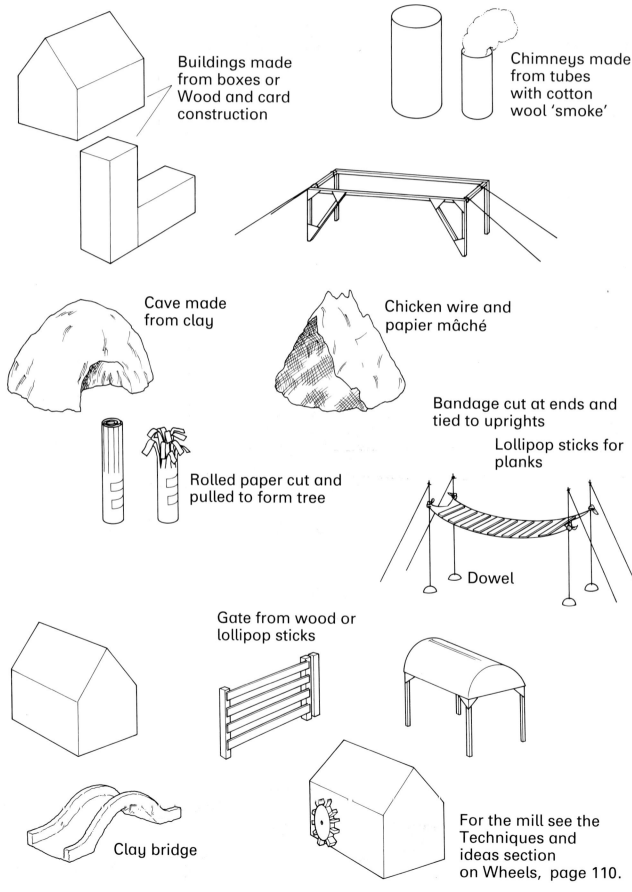

Out and about: Direction games

DIRECTIONS

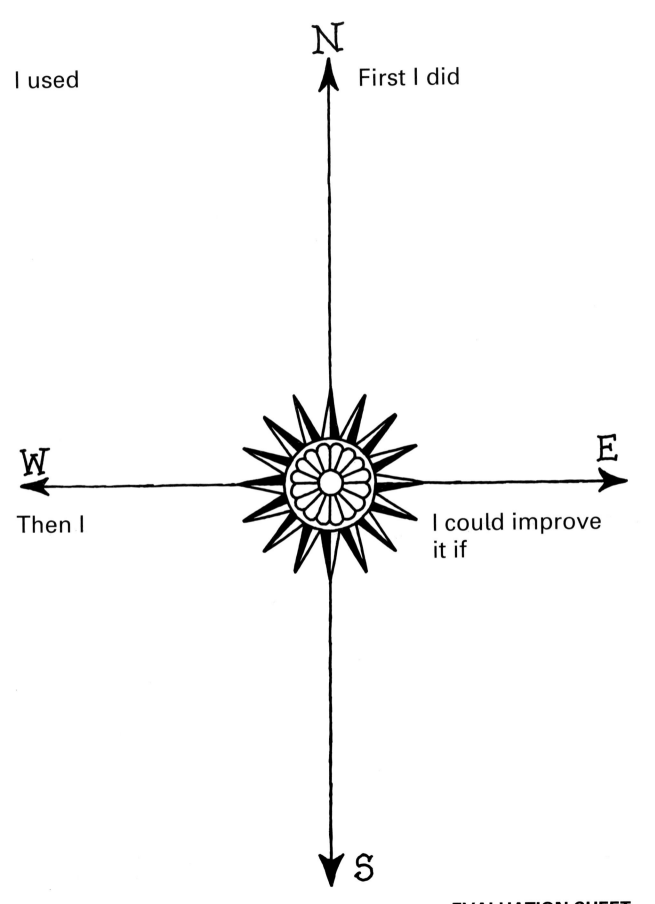

I used

First I did

Then I

I could improve it if

EVALUATION SHEET

Technology from stories

Stories of all sorts are an excellent starting point for Technology, particularly with Key Stage 1 children. Work can arise quite naturally from discussion about stories read in class and can develop the strong and important fantasy and imaginative element in young children's Technology work. The need that can arise from a discussion of the Three Little Pigs' search for strong house building materials will be just as real and important as one that derives from everyday life.

This section provides you with a bank of activities drawn from eight familiar stories for 5–7 year olds. You can use them both as an ideas bank in their own right or as examples of how to identify and develop exciting opportunities from a wide range of other books that you will read to your class over the course of any one year. Story technology is all around you. With this in mind we have included a bibliography of other common books in the infant class library which have substantial technological potential.

The eight stories covered in detail are:
Tumbledown
The Cow who fell in the Canal
The Mice and the Clockwork Bus
I don't want to live in a House
Phoebe and her Hot-Water Bottles
The Giant Jam Sandwich
Kit and the Magic Kite
The Enormous Crocodile

You will find a brief summary of each story and then a numbered list of suggested Technology activities that arise naturally from it. For each numbered activity you will then find detailed step-by-step ideas, which are often illustrated. You will find that these activities are cross-referenced throughout to techniques and ideas that are covered elsewhere in the book. It is not intended that the ideas are put directly in front of children as models to be made up, but rather are to be used flexibly by the teacher. The children themselves may suggest ideas for making models and solving problems. You will also find that many of the stories can be linked to other approaches to Technology, particularly topics, and the topic planner on page viii will help you to reference them in this way.

Technology from stories

Story 1

Tumbledown

Author
P. Rogers

Publisher
Walker Books, 1987

Summary of story
The village of Tumbledown is very run down and delapidated, nobody bothers and nothing ever gets repaired. One day, the news that a Prince was coming to visit sends the villagers into a panic. They rush round and mend everything. When the Prince arrives, he looks round the smart, carefully mended village but much prefers the ramshackle village hall that had not been mended at all.

Technology activities
1 Design and make a new church tower with a bell that rings.
2 Make a new gate for the school.
3 Design and make a new plank bridge to cross the stream.
4 Design and make a new village hall with strong steps.

Equipment/materials
Wood, card, dowel, empty boxes, string, masking tape, felt, hacksaw, ruler, glue, bobbins, small ball, plastic tubing, scissors, bench hook

1 A church tower with bell

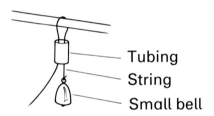

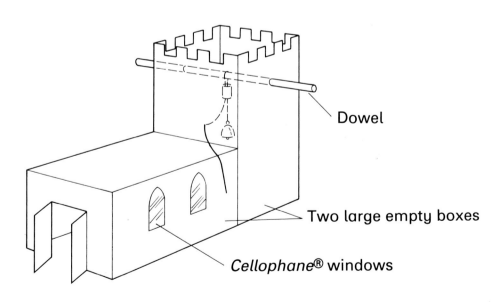

2 A gate

See page 95.

Technology from stories

3 A bridge

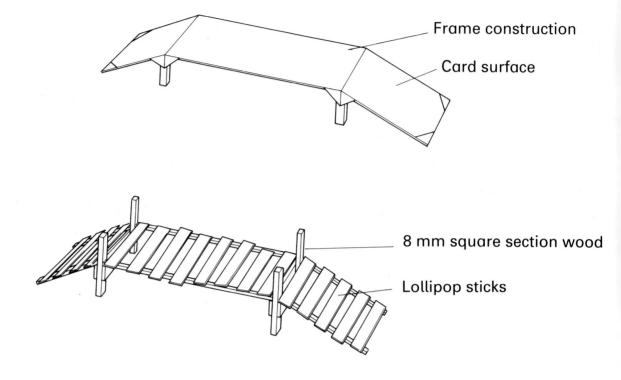

4 A village hall

For the building, see
Structures theme, Houses on
page 58.

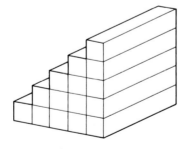

To make steps

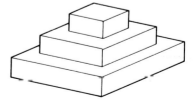

Graded boxes or 8 mm square
section wood strips cut to the
same length and glued
together.

Technology from stories

Story 2: The Cow who fell in the Canal

Author
P. Kraslovsky

Publisher
World's Work Ltd, 1958

Summary of story
Hendrika was an unhappy cow who longed to see the sights of the city and explore new places. One day whilst she was grazing, she fell into the canal. She managed to build a raft on which she floated down the river to the town. She happily explored the town until her owner caught up with her and took her home again – a wiser and happier cow!

Technology activities
1 Design and make the farmer's windmill.
2 Make Hendrika's raft.
3 Design and make a canal bridge to lower and raise.
4 Make some large cheese carriers.
5 Design and make some large scales for weighing cheeses.
6 Make Mr. Hofstra's market stall.
7 Make Pieter's wagon.
8 Make a gate to prevent Hendrika escaping.

Equipment/materials
8 mm square section wood, lollipop sticks, dowel, bobbins, rubber bands, card tubes, plastic bottles, string, glue, card, hand drill, hacksaw, benchhook, weights, hooks, wheels, hole punch

1 The farmer's windmill

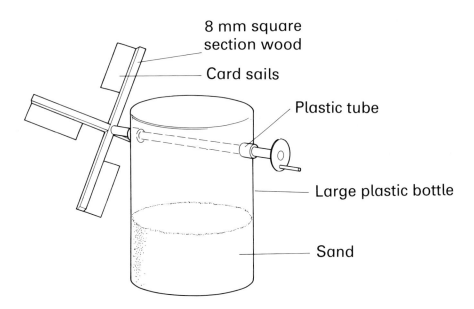

See also the Techniques and ideas section on Pulleys on page 115.

2 Hendrika's raft

Use 'wood and card' technique (see the Techniques and ideas section on page 108).

Waterproof the raft by varnishing or painting with PVA glue.

Technology from stories

3 The canal bridge

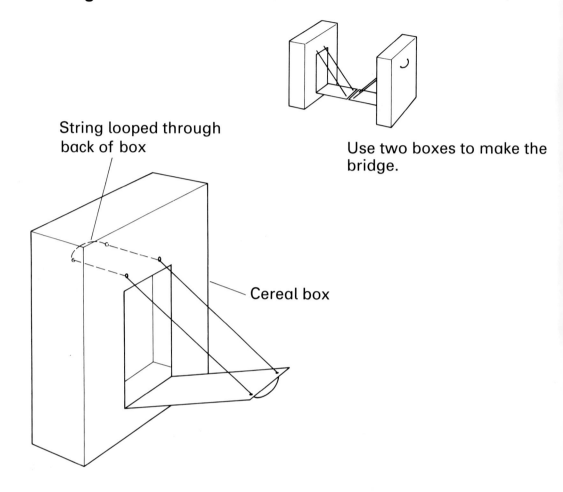

String looped through back of box

Use two boxes to make the bridge.

Cereal box

4 Cheese carriers

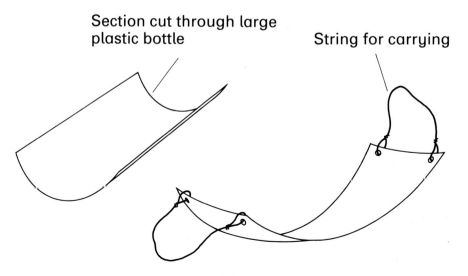

Section cut through large plastic bottle

String for carrying

Technology from stories

5 Scales for weighing cheeses

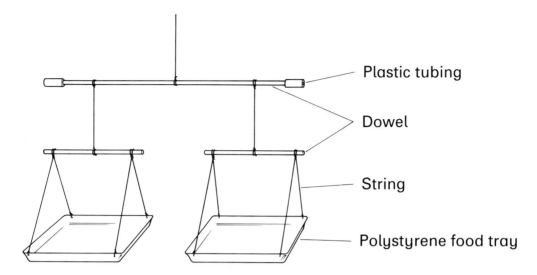

- Plastic tubing
- Dowel
- String
- Polystyrene food tray

See also the Techniques and ideas section on Pulleys on page 114.

6 Mr Hofstra's market stall

Use 'wood and card' technique (see the Techniques and ideas section on page 108).

7 Peter's wagon

See Movement theme, Vehicles on page 5.

8 A gate to stop Hendrika escaping

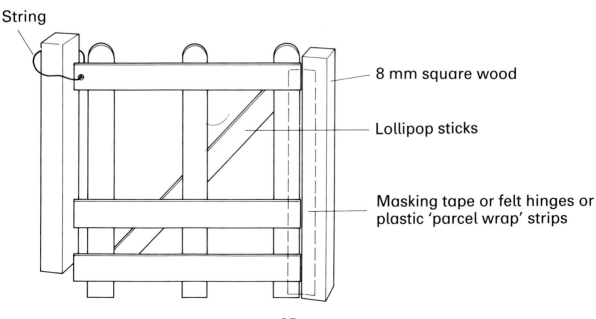

- String
- 8 mm square wood
- Lollipop sticks
- Masking tape or felt hinges or plastic 'parcel wrap' strips

Technology from stories

Story 3: The Mice and the Clockwork Bus

Author
Rodney Peppe

Publisher
Penguin Books, 1986

Summary of story
D. Rat, the greedy junk merchant runs a very inefficient bus-service for mice. Things go wrong so often that the mice decide to make some changes by building their own bus. Working together using old scrap materials, they build a wonderful clockwork bus. D. Rat is very unhappy and does his best to spoil things, including stealing the key to the bus. Eventually the villain is caught and is punished and the new bus-service operates without a hitch.

Technology activities
1 Make D. Rat's bus.
2 Make a shoe house where all the mice live.
3 Design and make a new bus for the mice.

Equipment/materials
Wood, card, dowel, glue, string, bobbins, rubber bands, matchsticks, foam-pipe lagging, old shoe/boot, empty boxes, card discs, wheels, cheese boxes, range of junk suitable for mouse bus

1   D Rat's bus

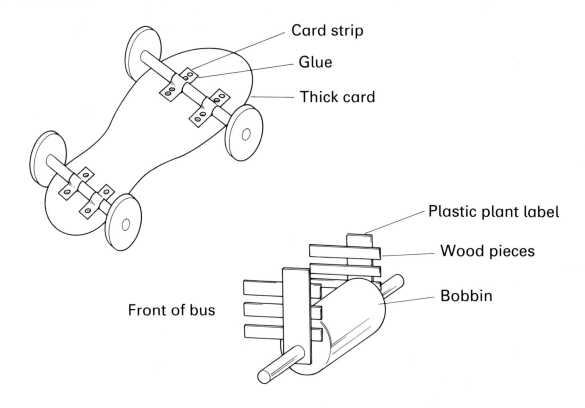

2   A shoe house

Use an old shoe, boot or PE slipper as a base and allow the children free choice of materials to build the house.

3   The mice's new bus

Using the illustrations in the book, offer the children a large range of junk materials. Encourage them to use techniques they have already learned.

Technology from stories

Story 4: I don't want to live in a house

Author
A. Jungmann & A. Axworthy

Publisher
W. Heinemann Ltd, 1987

Summary of story
Christopher's parents tell him they are going to buy a new house and ask him what kind of house he would like to live in. Christopher does not want to live in a house: he fancies a tent, an igloo, a tree house, a cave, or a raft! Eventually he realises a house would be best.

Technology activities
1. Make a tent.
2. Make a model igloo.
3. Design and make a model tree house.
4. Make and paint a cave.
5. Design and make a raft.

Equipment/materials
Fabric, straws, needles and thread, dowel, string, *Modroc*®, balloon, wood, plastic tubing, plastic bottles, card, hacksaw, hand drill, clay, masking tape, felt, ruler, glue, scissors, benchhook

1 A tent

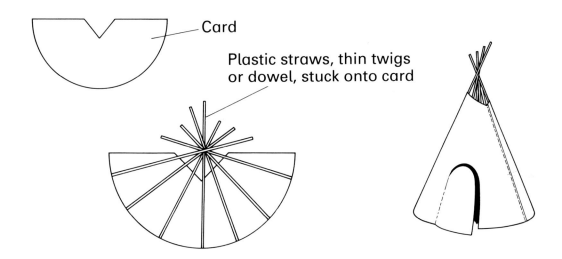

Card

Plastic straws, thin twigs or dowel, stuck onto card

2 An igloo

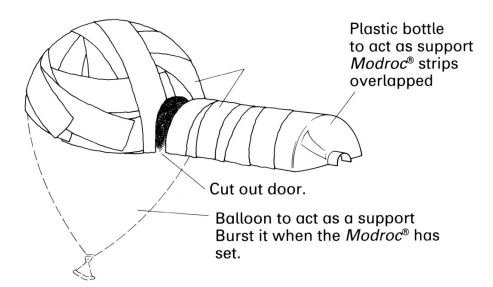

Plastic bottle to act as support
Modroc® strips overlapped

Cut out door.

Balloon to act as a support. Burst it when the *Modroc*® has set.

97

Technology from stories

3 A model tree-house

For the house see Structures theme, Houses on page 58

Find a suitable sized branch and secure it in a pot or container filled with pebbles to provide balance. Fasten the house into the branches using string.

4 A cave

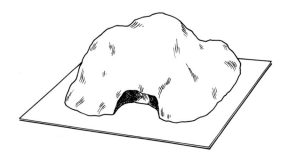

Clay, *Plasticine*® or papier mâché on base board.

5 A raft

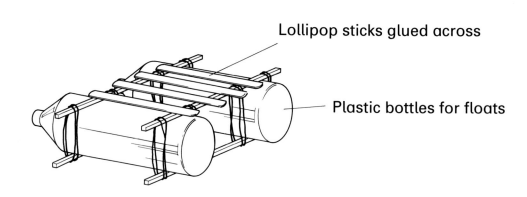

Lollipop sticks glued across

Plastic bottles for floats

Technology from stories

Story 5: Phoebe and her Hot-Water Bottles

Author
T. Furchgott & L. Dawson

Publisher
Picture Lions, 1977

Summary of story
Phoebe lives with her father, a busy chemist. Each Christmas and birthday he bought her a hot-water bottle as a present. Soon she had one hundred and fifty seven! They became her friends and companions, but she longed for a puppy. One night the shop caught fire. Phoebe, acting quickly, used the water from her hot water bottles to douse the fire. Her father realised she was a sensible child and gave her the puppy she had always wanted.

Technology activities
1 Design and make a 'shoe-box' shop.
2 Design and make a trolley to hold a real hot-water bottle.
3 Design and make a model of Pheobe's bed, including bedding and pillows.

Equipment/materials
Shoe box, card, wood, scissors, benchhook, hacksaw, ruler, glue, fabric and thread, needles, pins, paint, clay, string

1 A shoe-box shop

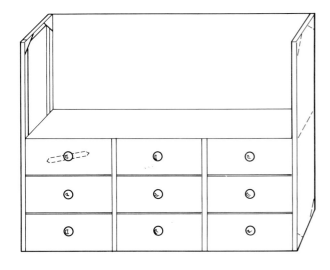

Matchbox drawers with paper-fastener handles.

a Remove one side of the shoe box.

b Reinforce the shoe box with 'wood and card' technique frame. See the Techniques and ideas section on page 108.

c Using card triangles, secure two pieces of wood across the box.

d Lay balsa or stiff card across the wood struts.

e Fill the shelf with model bottles etc.

99

Technology from stories

2 A hot-water bottle trolley

Use 'wood and triangle' technique. See Movement theme, Vehicles on page 5. Remember: hooks to fasten several vehicles together.

The trolley is to hold a real hot-water bottle.

Encourage the children to measure accurately.

A reinforced cereal box for the body of the vehicle.

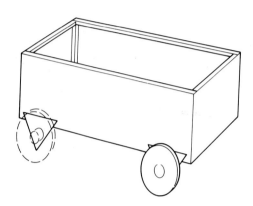

3 A model of Phoebe's bed

Use 'wood and card' technique. See the Techniques and ideas section on page 108.

When designing and making bedding, remember to use appropriate fabrics which are flame retardant.

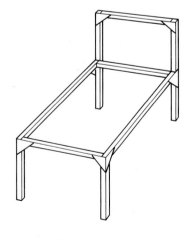

Technology from stories

Story 6: The Giant Jam Sandwich

Author
J. V. Lord & J. Burroway

Publisher
Jonathan Cape Ltd.

Summary of the story
Millions of wasps cause chaos in Itching Down, so the villagers decide to make a giant jam sandwich to trap the wasps. A huge loaf is made and transported to the fields where it is sliced and spread thickly with jam. The greedy wasps swoop on the jam and are trapped in the sandwich, leaving Itching Down peaceful again.

1 A loaf of bread

a Encourage the children to estimate before weighing their ingredients.

b Make sure the loaf is a realistic size for making a transporter.

2 A bread transporter

Use 'wood and card' technique (see the Techniques and ideas section on page 108).

3 A table-cloth

For the table-cloth consider size, shape, aesthetic appearance and suitable fabrics.

Technology activities
1 Make a loaf of bread.
2 Design and make a vehicle to transport the loaf (the vehicle must be appropriate to the size of the real loaf).
3 Make a table-cloth on which to place the loaf of bread.
4 Design and make
  a a tip-up lorry to carry the jam.
  b a bull-dozer to spread the butter.
  c a wheelbarrow to carry the jam.
5 Design and make a flying machine.

Equipment/materials
Bread mix ingredients, wood, card, wheels, glue, dowel, string, punch, plastic tubing, fabric, thread, scissors, needles, syringe, plastic bottle, bobbins, matchbox, plastic plant labels, hack-saw, benchhooks

4 A tip-up lorry, bulldozer and wheelbarrow

a A tip-up lorry

See Movement theme, Vehicles that carry a load on pages 6, 7.

b A bulldozer

See Structures theme, Building Site vehicles to make a bulldozer, on page 71.

c A wheelbarrow

See Movement theme, Vehicles that are easy to make on page 14.

5 A flying machine

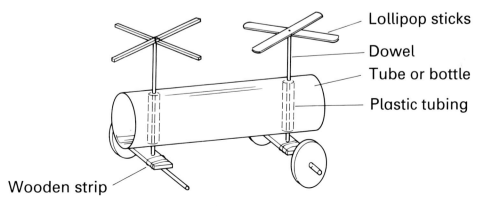

101

Technology from stories

Story 7: Kit and the Magic Kite

Author
Helen Cooper

Publisher
Hamish Hamilton 1987

Summary of story
Kit the cat wanted to see the big wide world. The magic yellow kite takes him on a far-away journey. Kit tried being an alley-cat and a fierce wild-cat but neither was for him. The kite took him across the ocean so that Kit could try being a ship's cat but that was not much fun either. Kit then tried being a witch's cat but that was too scarey. Kit decided he preferred living in his own land, in his own garden! His friend the magic kite finally took him home where he shared his adventures with neighbouring cats.

Technology activities
1. Make the ginger cat.
2. Make the magic yellow kite.
3. Make a fishing boat with sails.
4. Make the hold of the boat, fill it with sacks, boxes and tubs and make a ladder to enter the hold.
5. Make the witch's house.

Equipment/materials
Orange furry fabric, needle, thread, glue, scissors, felt, yellow tissue paper, string, dowel, 8 mm wood, card, hand-drill, hessian material, lollipop sticks, pasta, lentils, beans, boxes, tubes

1 Kit the ginger cat

See Movement theme, Moving toys on page 18 to make a glove-puppet cat.

2 The magic yellow kite

See Out and About theme, Holidays on making a kite on page 80.

3 A fishing boat with sails

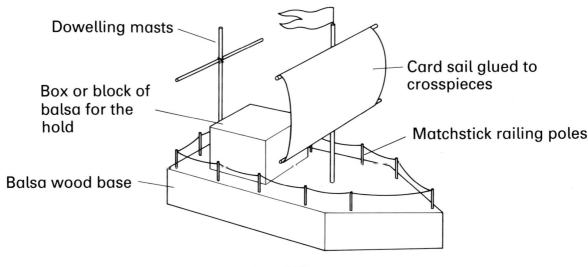

102

Technology from stories

4 The hold of the boat

a Use a cardboard box for the ship's hold.

b Make sacks from hessian and stuff with tissues.

c Two hessian rectangles, stitched on three sides then turned inside out

d Finally over-sew the top of the sack.

e Make tubs and boxes from junk.

f Make the ladder using wood and lollipop sticks.

See Structures theme, Houses on page 63 to make bunk beds.

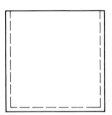 

5 The witch's house

a Use 'wood and card' triangle technique (see the Techniques and Ideas section on page 108 to make the witch's house.

b Make the walls and roof from card and glue on to wooden frame.

c Decorate walls and roof with pasta shapes, beans, lentils etc. glued firmly with PVA glue.

Paint as necessary.

Technology from stories

Story 8

The Enormous Crocodile

Author
Roald Dahl

Publisher
Jonathan Cape, 1978.

Summary of story
The greedy, wicked enormous crocodile leaves his river to go and find a little child to eat for lunch. He meets all the animals in the jungle and horrifies them with his plans. At last he sees some children and tries to trick them with disguises. Each time he is foiled by the jungle animals who warn the children. His last attempt to trick the children ends in disaster, Trunky the elephant is on hand to help the children – he grabs the wicked crocodile by the tail and flings him far out into space. The enormous crocodile is never seen again.

Technology activities
1 Make the enormous crocodile.
2 Make the fairground
   a a helter-skelter
   b a roundabout
   c a see-saw
   d swings.

Equipment/materials
Card, scissors, glue, paper, corriflute, wood, cardboard, needles and thread, clay, benchhook, hacksaw, chicken wire, newspaper, clothes pegs, pinking shears

1 The Crocodile

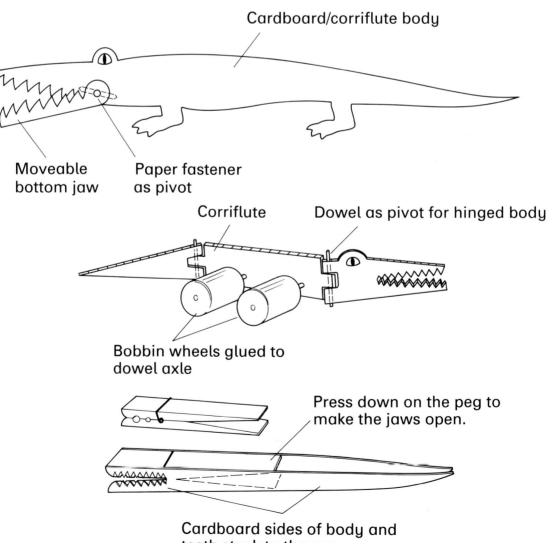

104

Technology from stories

2 The fairground

a A helter-skelter

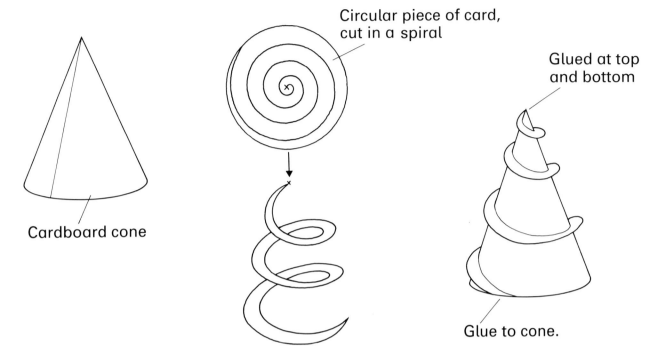

b A roundabout

See Out and About theme, Holidays, to make a model roundabout on page 79.

c and d See-saw and swings

See Taking Care of Things theme, Playground to make model swings and a see-saw on page 51.

Technology from stories

Other stories to use

Author	Title	Publisher
Eve Rice	Ten Tales from Aesop	Fontana
Gerald Ross	Ahhh! said stork	Young Lions
Jenny Wagner	Aranea 'A Story about a Spider'	Kestrel Books
Bill Peet	Big Bad Bruce	Andre Deutsch
Margaret Stuart Barry	Boffey & The Teacher Eater (in 'Our Best Stories')	Knight Books
Roald Dahl	Charlie & The Chocolate Factory	Puffin
Roald Dahl	Charlie Needs a Cloak	Puffin
Judi Barell	Cloudy with a Chance of Meatballs	W. S. Cowell Ltd.
Roald Dahl	Danny the Champion of the World	Puffin
Edward Ardizzone	Diana and Her Rhinoceros	Bodley Head
Michael Foreman	Dinosaurs and all that Rubbish	Picture Puffins
Annie M. G. Schmidt	Dusty and Smudge and the Soap Suds	A Methuen Starting Book
McKee	Elmer the Patchwork Elephant	Pan Piccolo Books
Fisk Barker	Emma Borrows a Cup of Sugar	Heinemann
R. J. Stephens	Faster than Anything	Ernest Bann
Raymond Briggs	Fungus the Bogeyman	Hamish Hamilton
Roald Dahl	Gran's Marvellous Medicine	Puffin
Edward Ardizzone	Johnny the Clock Maker	Oxford University
Ann Mari Falk	Matthew Blows Soap Bubbles	Burke
Mollie Clark	Mink and the Fire (First Folk Tales)	Rupert-Hart Davis
Yeoman/Blake	Mouse Trouble	Hamish Hamilton
Pamela Allen	Mr. Archimede's Bath	Bodley Head
Shizuko Kurantoni	Mr. Bear and Apple Jam	MacDonald
Michael Bond	Mr. Cramar's Magic Bubbles	Picture Puffin
Elisa Trimby	Mr. Plum's Oasis	Faber & Faber
Zolotov	Mr. Rabbit and the Lovely Present	Picture Puffin
Christopher Masters	Mr. Tulip Grinds to a Halt	Frederick Warne
Alf Proysen	Mrs. Pepperpot's Busy Day	Hutchinson
Catherine Starr	Polly and the Stupid Wolf	Young Puffin
Vera Southgate	Rapunzel	Ladybird
Elizabeth Levy	Spinning in Space	
Bechis	Teddy and the Seesaw	Methuen & Co. Ltd.
Eric Carle	The Badtempered Ladybird	Picture Puffins
E & G Rose	The Big River	Faber & Faber
Max Valthuys	The Boy and the Kite	Black
Margaret Mary	The Boys with Two Shadows	J. M. Dent
M. F. Bartlett	The Clean Brook	A & C Black
	The Double Colour 1, 2, 3 Book	Perpetua Press
	The Double Colour ABC Book	Perpetua Press
Dell Britt	The Emperor's Big Gift	A World's Work Children's Book
Vera Southgate	The Gingerbread Boy	Ladybird
Eva Marder	The Hedgehog Muron	Blackie
Ted Hughes	The Iron Man	Faber & Faber
Edward Lear	The Jumblies (Book of Nonsense by R. L. Green)	J. M. Dent & Sons
B. Wildsmith	The Lazy Bear	Oxford University
Armitage	The Lighthouse Keeper's Lunch	Andre Deutsch
Chrislenson/Hollander	The Magic Clock	Frederick Warne
William Crookes	The Magic Paper Boat	Carousel
David McKee	The Magician & The Balloon	Abelard
Tomi Ungerer	The Mellops Go Flying	Methuen & Co. Ltd.
Papas	The Monk and the Goat	Oxford University

Useful techniques and ideas

This section contains 11 photocopiable sheets of techniques and ideas which are invaluable for Key Stage 1. They are intended primarily for teacher use, but there may be occasions when you want to give out a sheet for children to work with on their own. The techniques in this section cover basic work on frames, wheels, pulleys, cogs, gears and electricity. They are intended as a basic vocabulary of useful core skills which will be used to solve particular problems in a range of different contexts. You will find these techniques widely referred to in other sections. You will probably want to introduce these techniques to children in a particular context to solve a particular problem. Once they have mastered a technique the children should be encouraged to use it widely in a variety of situations.

The techniques are as follows:

1 Basic frameworks 1

2 Basic frameworks 2

These sheets introduce the widely used 'Jinks technique' for making strong simple structures out of card and wood. Use small section wood and PVA glue. These simple frameworks are very strong and can be used widely, for example to make models of buildings, bridges and vehicles.

3 Wheels

4 Giving grip to wheels

A simple introduction to different kinds of homemade wheels.

5 Spacers and end stops for axles

6 Fastening wheels and axles to chassis

Used in conjunction with sheets 1–4, these sheets will enable children to construct their own wheeled vehicles.

7 Simple pulleys

8 Using simple pulleys

A guide to making and using pulleys in simple models.

9 Cogs and gears

These cogs and gears can be used when making models with moving parts.

10 Joining ideas

These joining ideas will have a wide range of uses. Once mastered, children can apply these techniques independently to the models.

11 Electricity

This sheet introduces the very basics of electricity, circuits and switches for infant children. You can extend this work to introduce children to other simple switches such as pressure pads.

Useful techniques and ideas

Basic frameworks 1

To make a right-angled corner

Use card triangles and wood.

Cut card triangles from ruled squares.

Glue triangle onto wood.

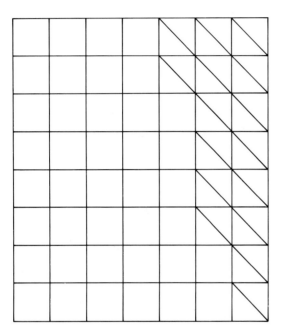

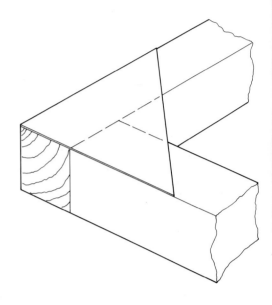

To make an upright corner

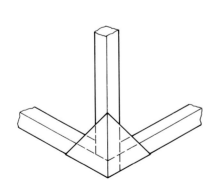

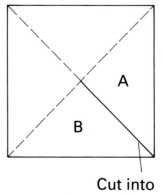

Cut into card square.

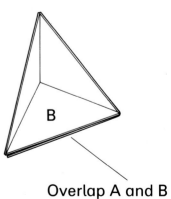

Overlap A and B like this.

Basic frameworks 2

To make a joint

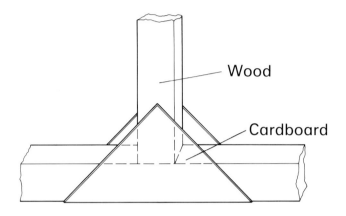

To attach an axle

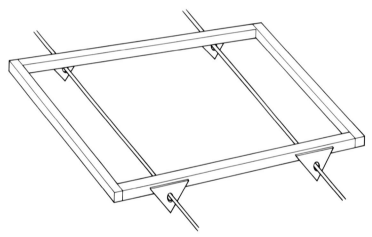

Card triangles with holes punched in glued to frame

To make a cube

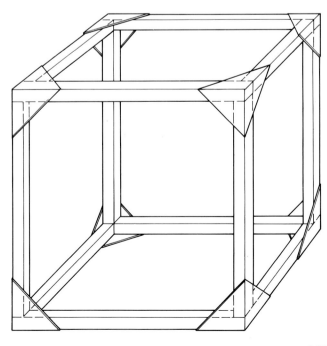

Useful techniques and ideas

Wheels

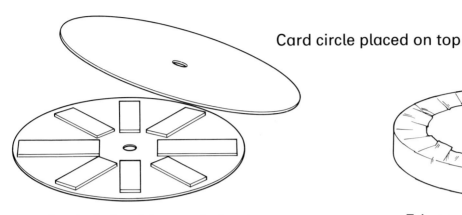

Card circle placed on top

Card circle with wood glued on (lollipop sticks can be used.)

Edge covered with masking tape cut and folded over

Other wheels

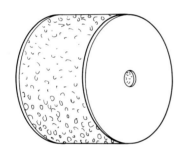

Card circles and foam insulating tube

Card discs glued to centre from *sellotape*® reel

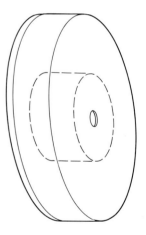

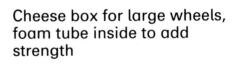

Cheese box for large wheels, foam tube inside to add strength

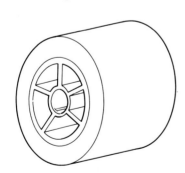

Bobbin inside foam pipe lagging or insulating tube

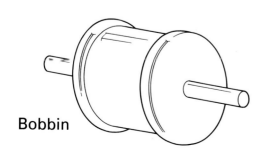

Bobbin

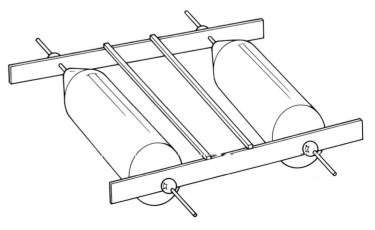

Washing-up bottle wheels

110

Useful techniques and ideas

Giving grip to wheels

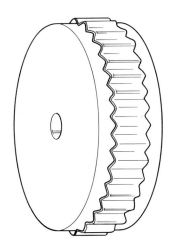

Corrugated cardboard strip

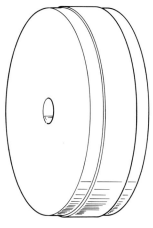

Wide rubber band

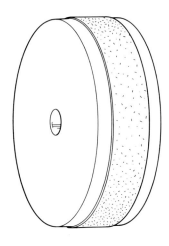

Strip of sandpaper

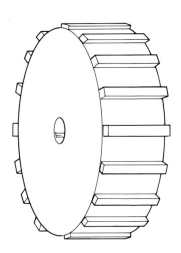

Matchsticks glued to card strip at regular intervals (suitable for tractor)

Useful techniques and ideas

Spacers and end stops for axles

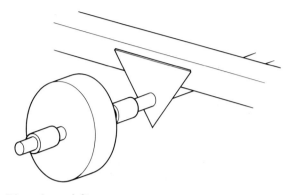

Plastic tubing

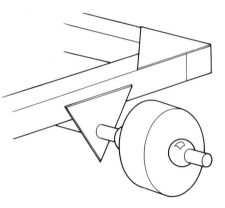

Small beads

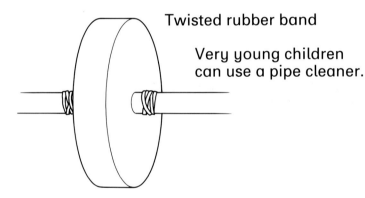

Twisted rubber band

Very young children can use a pipe cleaner.

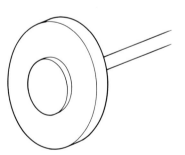

Circle of rigid cardboard stuck over axle hole.

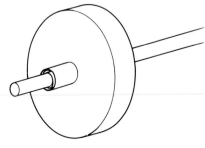

Narrow strip of paper wrapped round several times and glued

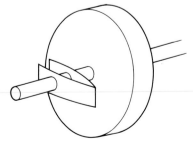

Thin piece of plastic washing-up bottle cut and punched

Useful techniques and ideas

Techniques 6: Fastening wheels and axles to a chassis

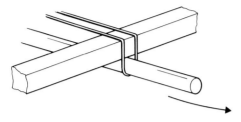

Axles and wheels secured to frame with rubber band

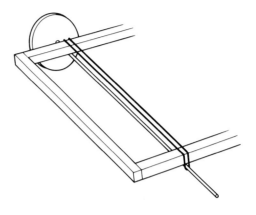

Axles pass through corrugated plastic sheeting

Useful techniques and ideas

Simple pulleys

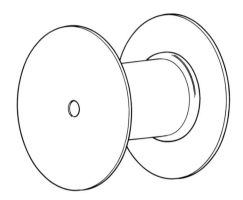

Two card circles glued to a bobbin

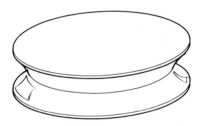

Glue two deep tin lids together.

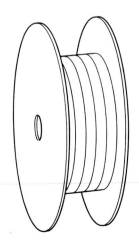

Four to six small card circles glued together between two larger card discs

Useful techniques and ideas

Using simple pulleys

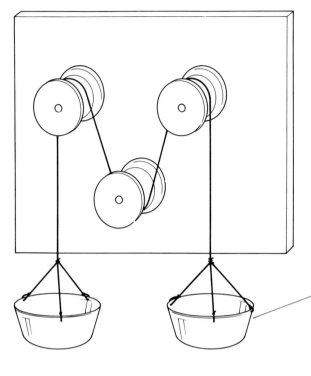

Cotton bobbin pulleys attached to board with dowel provide a simple balance

Plastic tubs with string threaded through

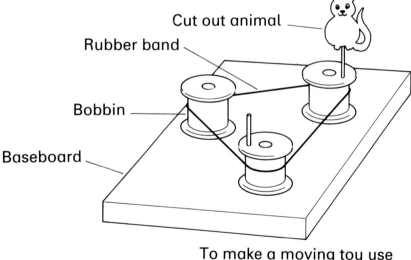

Cut out animal

Rubber band

Bobbin

Baseboard

To make a moving toy use bobbins placed on a piece of dowel. A handle made from dowel can be glued onto the bobbin.

This simple windmill turns with a pulley made from bobbins and an elastic band.

Useful techniques and ideas

Cogs and gears

Techniques 9

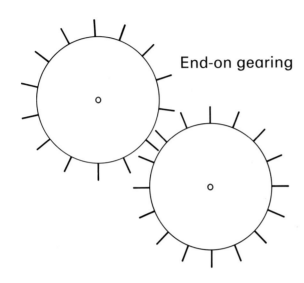

End-on gearing

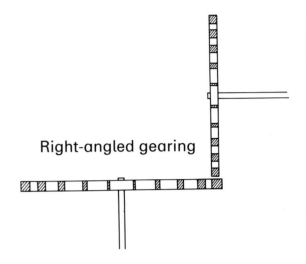

Right-angled gearing

To make cogs

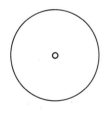

Card circles

Lollipop sticks

Equal length pieces of 8 mm square wood

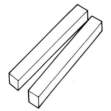

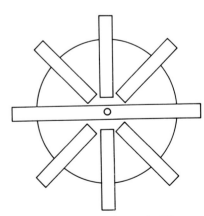

Glue wood to card. Place second circle on top.

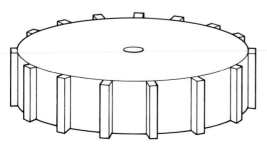

Wheel edged with thick corrugated card or card with matchsticks stuck on

116

Useful techniques and ideas

Joining ideas

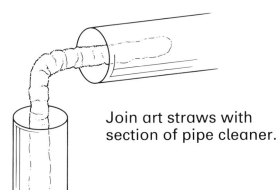

Join art straws with section of pipe cleaner.

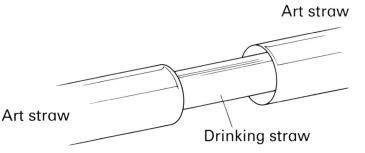

Art straw

Art straw

Drinking straw

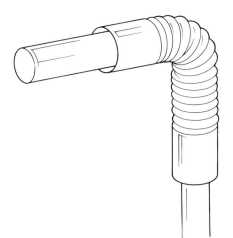

Join dowel with bendy straws. You may need a spot of glue on the end of the dowel.

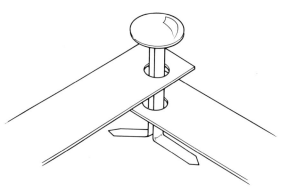

Fasten card or plastic strips with split-pin paper fasteners.

Plastic tubing

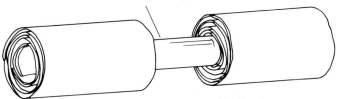

Rolled newspaper can be extended with a piece of plastic tubing.

Useful techniques and ideas

Electricity

Simple circuits

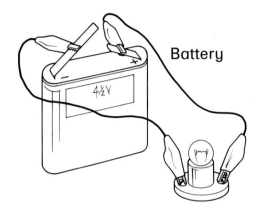

Battery

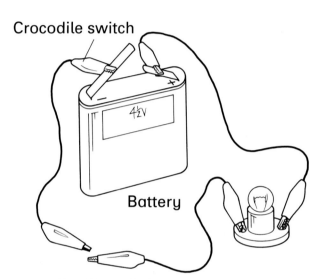

Crocodile switch

Battery

Crocodile clip switch

Simple switches

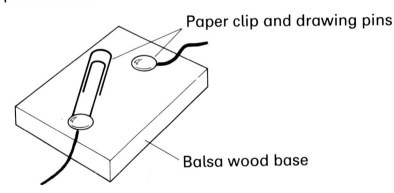

Paper clip and drawing pins

Balsa wood base

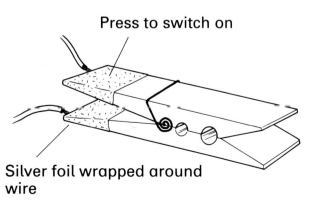

Press to switch on

Silver foil wrapped around wire

Challenges

The aim of this section is to provide a bank of challenges that children can use independently and largely without adult help. Each activity has a specific focus and sets the children a realistic challenge within a clearly defined structure, (e.g. Can you make a Jack-in-the-box?) Across the set of challenges, children will need to use a variety of the skills and techniques that have been introduced throughout the book.

We suggest that the challenges can both be used to extend children's thinking and also to consolidate learning from previous topic work or activities.

The challenges will fit readily into any classroom organisation, and will allow children to pursue a worthwhile Technology activity without requiring significant teacher input. There is scope for a child to interpret the challenge in his or her own way and to use imagination and creativity to achieve an individual result.

These challenges are ideal for co-operative work. Children can work in pairs or small groups to tackle a challenge. It may be helpful to initially introduce the challenge to the children and develop their ideas through questioning (Does the Jack-in-the-box need to look like the one in the picture?) The children should then be encouraged to discuss their ideas and plan together how they will approach the challenge. A design sheet could also be used (page 144) to provide a working tool for the group.

The activities suggested by the challenges, require children to have access to a range of simple resources (tools, junk etc – see page 140) but you may wish to make them more difficult or more specific by restricting the materials that the children can use. (e.g. Can you make a Jack-in-the-box without using wood?)

In order to extend the challenge activities, children could be asked to research ideas and background; for example, children could be asked to look at a baby's rattle and consider it in detail before making one.

Can you make a Jack-in-the-box?

You might use some of these:

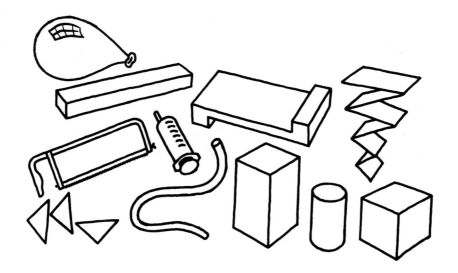

Think about:

how to make the cube.

how Jack will jump up.

how to make Jack.

what Jack is fastened to.

Challenges 1

Can you make a money box?

You might use some of these:

Think about:

what to make your money box from.

how to get your money out.

where to put your money in.

Will your money box stand up?

Challenges 2

Can you make a vehicle with wobbly wheels?

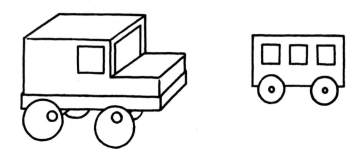

You might use some of these:

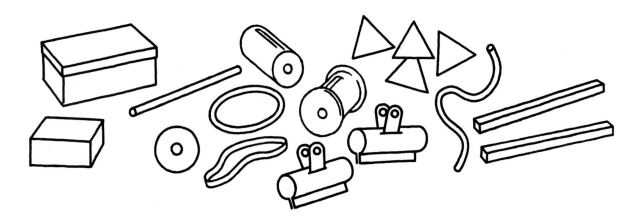

Think about:

what to use for wheels.

where to put the wheels.

how to fasten the wheels on.

Challenges 3

Can you make a crane to lift a 100 grammes?

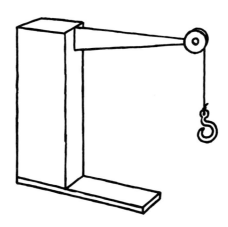

You might use some of these:

Think about:

how to make sure the crane doesn't fall over.

how to fasten the arm onto the crane.

how to lift the weight. Perhaps you could use a pulley.

Challenges 4

Can you make a tent big enough for you to get inside?

You might use some of these:

Think about:

how to fasten your frame together.

what to make your tent from.

how to fasten the material to the frame

Will it stand up?

Challenges 5

Can you make a box to open and close with a magnet?

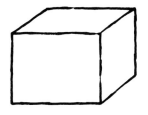
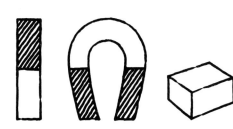

You might use some of these:

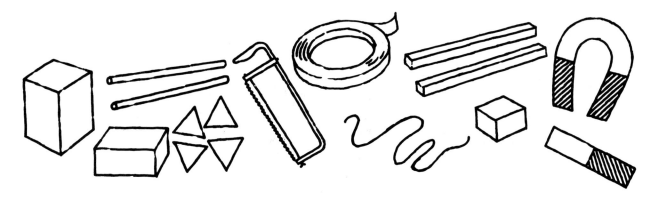

Think about:

why you will need two magnets.

how you will fasten a magnet to the box.

Is your box strong enough?

Challenges 6

Can you make a table game with a track that uses two dice?

Perhaps you can make the dice too.

You might use some of these:

Think about:

what to make the board from.

how to play the game.

what the rules are

what to use for counters.

Challenges 7

Can you make a puppet theatre?

You might use some of these:

Think about:

where to put the puppets.

Do you want curtains? How will you fasten them?

How big does the theatre need to be?

Challenges 8

Can you make a robot with eyes that light up?

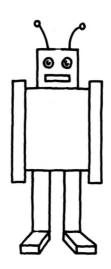

You might use some of these:

Think about:

how to fasten your robot together.

how to make a circuit. Do you need a switch?

Challenges 9

Can you make a football stadium with lights?

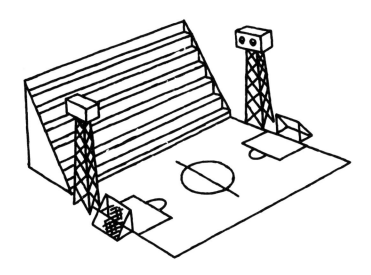

You might use some of these:

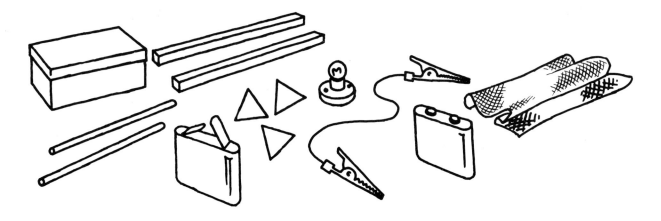

Think about:

how to make the stand.

what to use for the goals.

how to make the lights stand.

how to make the lights work.

Challenges 10

Can you make a baby's rattle?

You might use some of these:

Think about:

What to use to make the 'rattle' noise.

how the baby can hold it.

Is it safe for a baby to use?

Challenges 11

Can you make a bridge to stretch between two tables?

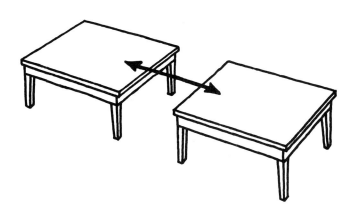

You might use some of these:

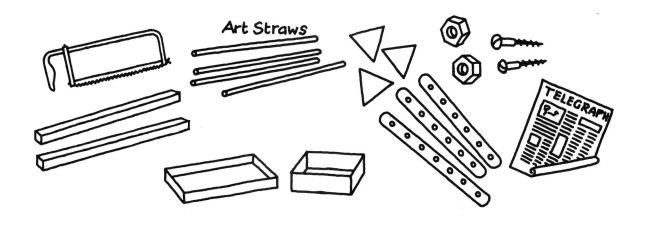

Think about:

what to make the bridge from.

how you can make the bridge strong (so that it will not bend in the middle).

whether the bridge is long enough.

Challenges 12

Can you make a musical instrument with strings?

You might use some of these:

Think about:

the size of the instrument.

how long the strings will be.

how to fasten the strings on.

Are the strings tight?

Challenges 13

Can you make a container for pencils, crayons etc?

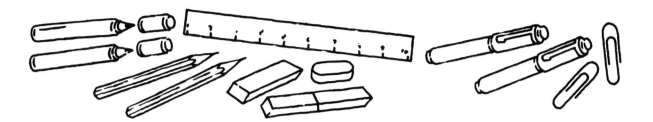

You might use some of these:

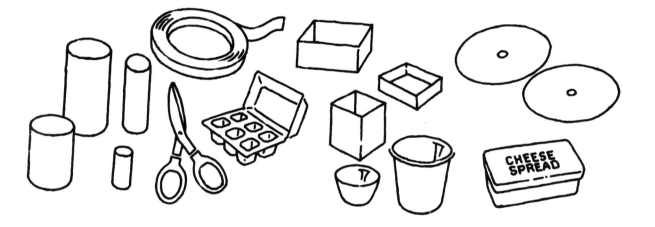

Think about:

thin and thick crayons, tall rulers and small rubbers.

how to make the container stand up when it is full and when it is empty.

Challenges 14

Can you make a face with moving parts?

You might use some of these:

Think about:

which parts will move – eyes? ears? nose?

how the parts will move.

Challenges 15

Can you make a school sign to welcome visitors

You might use some of these:

Think about:

The size of your sign and the size of the lettering.

how to fasten your sign to the door or wall.

what you need to put on your sign.

Challenges 16

Can you make a tower that is 1 metre tall

You might use some of these:

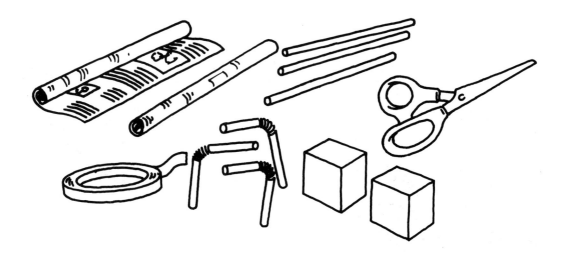

Think about:

how to make your tower strong.

how you will join things together.

Where to make your tower so that you don't have to move it.

Challenges 17

Can you make an alphabet mobile that spells your name?

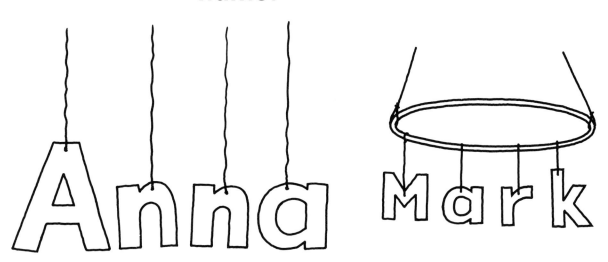

You might use some of these:

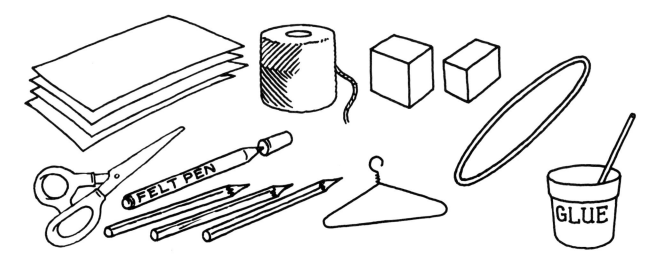

Think about:

the size of the letters.

how to hang the letters in the right order.

how to hang your mobile up.

Challenges 18

Can you make a model shopping trolley?

You might use some of these:

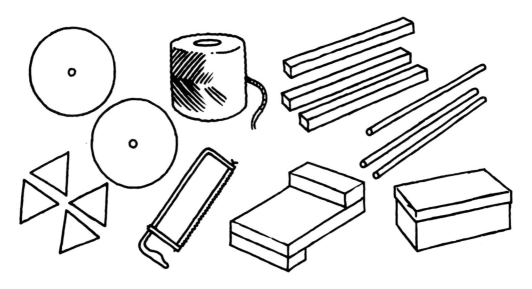

Think about:

how to make the trolley move.

space for the shopping - is the trolley strong enough?

how to fasten the handle.

Challenges 19

Resources and records

This section provides a short compendium of ideas and information which will be useful to you when organising and delivering Technology work in the classroom. It consists of the following:

Checklist of classroom equipment and materials
We have included a short and realistic list of the kinds of tools, materials and equipment that every infant class should look to provide. Many of these can be collected free, and junk materials could be provided by parents on a systematic basis.

Storage ideas
Access to equipment and materials is extremely important if children are to work independently. So is tidiness! It is therefore worth giving time and thought to classroom storage and organisation. We have included two pages of visual ideas for creating cheap, effective and neat storage devices in the classroom.

Once you have established an effective storage system, it is important to train children to understand and use it properly, so that they manage it rather than you. You can put children in charge of 'stock control', letting you know when you are running low on anything.

Designing
A sheet has been provided for children to record their own design briefs. You will find detailed information on using this on page 143.

Technology attainment target record
We have included a simple form for you to record information about children's National Curriculum experiences.

Programme of Study record sheets
Record sheets for children's experience of the Programmes of Study are also included.

CHECKLIST OF CLASSROOM EQUIPMENT AND MATERIALS

Basic classroom equipment

Hacksaws and spare blades
Simple hand drill and stand
Rulers
Scissors
Glue spreaders and glue pots
Magnets of various sorts
Small screw drivers
Batteries (various sorts) and battery holders
Bulbs and bulb holders
Plastic covered electric wire
Crocodile clips
Switches
Bench hooks

Basic classroom materials

Plastic tubing of varying diameters
Art straws
Range of children's glue
Paper clips, bull-dog clips and split-pin paper fasteners
Card and paper
Masking tape
Elastic bands: a range of lengths
String and thread, fishing line
Plastic syringes
Pipe cleaners

Plasticine®
Plaster of Paris and *Modroc*®
Marbles
Drawing pins
Dowel of various lengths and thickness
8 mm square section wood
Balloons
Lollipop sticks and matchsticks
Cup hooks
Beads and corks
Felt pens and painting pens
Paint, chalks, pastels, pencils etc
Cardboard wheels
Buttons
Thin wire (suitable for a young child to bend)

Basic junk materials

Plastic bottles of various sizes
Plastic straws, bendy straws and drinking straws
Aluminium foil
Cotton reels, rollers
Range of empty boxes, lids, containers and tubes
Coat hangers
Polystyrene blocks
Scraps of felt, wool, and a range of fabric scraps
Scrap card and board (ex-window display card is often good and also free!)

STORAGE IDEAS ▶

1 Individual storage basket for child to carry equipment safely from storage point to working area. It contains equipment for two children:

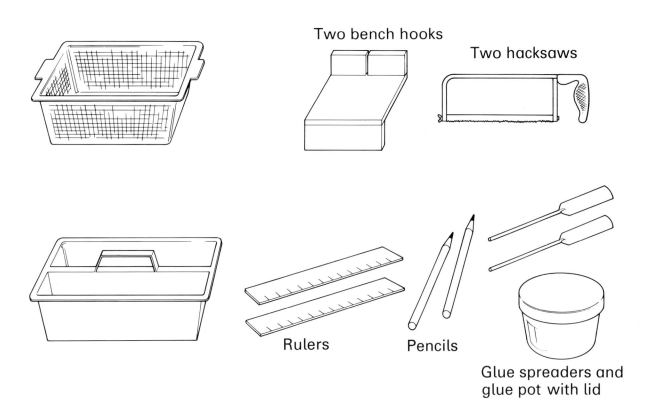

Two bench hooks

Two hacksaws

Rulers

Pencils

Glue spreaders and glue pot with lid

2 Storage of materials using stackable plastic vegetable racks

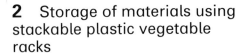

Holds bobbins, corks, wheels etc.

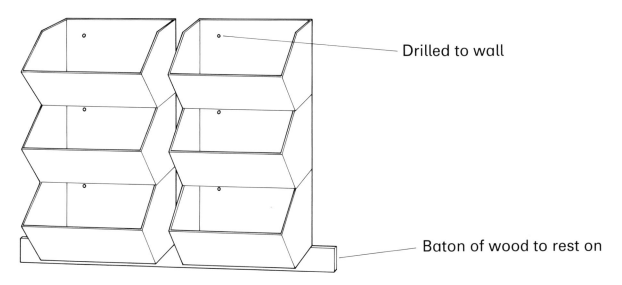

Drilled to wall

Baton of wood to rest on

STORAGE IDEAS

3 Storage of wood and 'junk' materials

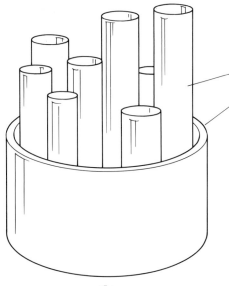

Junk cylinders and tubes stored in large card drum or old waste paper basket

Store wood strips and dowel inside large junk tubes or old plastic bottles.

Wood

Cylinder

Wine rack

Store tubes, bottles in wooden wine rack

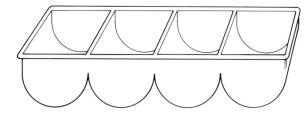

Plastic 'school' cutlery tray for batteries, bulbs, clips, etc.

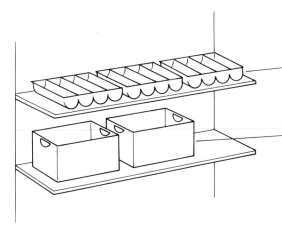

Lay trays end-to-end on low shelf to provide easy access for children.

Store other junk in plastic storage boxes under the shelf.

DESIGNING

The design process

The design stage is a vital part of Technology and children should always be encouraged to design before making.

For young children it is an important process that involves the transfer from 2D to 3D and the translation of ideas into reality. It will develop skills and concepts across the curriculum, particularly Mathematics, with an awareness of shape, experience of estimation and the development of proportion and scale. Children will develop language skills through discussion of ideas, development of relevant vocabulary and the ability to describe their work to others.

Children will need experiences upon which to build their designs; these might be first-hand experiences, visits to relevant places, looking at 3-D models, photographs, reference books etc.

Implications for the teacher

Children will need access to ideas source material, visits and first-hand experiences wherever possible. Children will need space – often large pieces of paper are used first. Children should be encouraged to cooperate, to share and discuss ideas with others, (both children and adults).

Be ready to step in and question the child about his/her design, asking for an explanation about how it will work. Encourage the child to look carefully at his/her design and improve it where possible. Relate the design to the practicalities of making it. Encourage the child to view his/her model from various angles; front, rear, above and below as well as from the side.

Consider where the child can put his/her design so as to be able to use it when making the model. (A bulldog clip hooked on to the wall above the child's worktop might be a good idea).

Ensure that a wide range of resources is available to meet the needs of the child's design.

Things for children to consider when designing

What will my model/end product look like?
How big will it be?
How will it move/turn/balance etc?
How will I fasten it together?
What will I use to make it?
Will it do what I want it to?

Design sheets

A photocopiable design sheet is included for children to use. This may need to be enlarged for some children. As a child works through a topic, his/her design sheets can be kept and stored together to form part of his/her Record of Achievement, to be shared with parents and provide evidence of the child's technology work.

My design for

This is what it will
look like

This is what I will use

Name

TECHNOLOGY ATTAINMENT RECORD

Name ....

Introduced
Experienced
Understood

AT \ Level	Level 1	Level 2	Level 3
1 Needs and opportunities			
2 Design			
3 Plan and make			
4 Evaluate			

145

Programme of Study Record Sheet 1	Movement	Changes	Taking Care of Things	Structures	Out and About
Level 1 Developing and using artefacts, systems and environments Pupils should be taught to:					
● know that a system is made of related parts which are combined for a purpose;					
● identify the jobs done by parts of a system;					
● give a sequence of instructions to produce a desired result;					
● recognise, and make models of, simple structures around them;					
● use sources of energy to make things move;					
● identify what should be done and ways in which work should be organised.					
Working with materials Pupils should be taught to:					
● explore and use a variety of materials to design and make things;					
● recognise that materials are processed in order to change or control their properties;					
● recognise that many materials are available and have different characteristics which make them appropriate for different tasks;					
● join materials and components in simple ways;					
● use materials and equipment safely.					
Developing and communicating ideas Pupils should be taught to:					
● use imagination, and their own experiences, to generate and explore ideas;					
● represent and develop ideas by drawings, models, talking, writing, working with materials;					
● find out, sort, store and present information for use in designing and making.					

Programme of Study Record Sheet 2	Movement	Changes	Taking Care of Things	Structures	Out and About
Level 1 (continued) Satisfying needs and addressing opportunities Pupils should be taught to:					
● know that goods are bought, sold and advertised;					
● realise that resources are limited, and choices must be made;					
● evaluate their finished work against the original intention.					
Developing and using artefacts, systems and environments In addition pupils working towards level 1 should be taught to:					
● recognise that materials can be linked in various ways to make or allow movement;					
● make simple objects for a purpose.					
Satisfying needs and addressing opportunities					
● talk about what they have done during their designing and making;					
● evaluate familiar things by observing and describing them, saying what they like or dislike about them and why people have or need them.					
Level 2 Developing and using artefacts, systems and environments In addition pupils working towards level 2 should be taught to:					
● recognise that control involves making things work as desired.					
Working with materials					
● Choose materials and equipment to make objects;					
● investigate the properties of materials in the course of their designing and making;					
● identify natural and manufactured materials;					
● use simple hand tools, and know how to look after them;					

Programme of Study Record Sheet 3	Movement	Changes	Taking Care of Things	Structures	Out and About
Level 2 (continued) ● care for their surroundings.					
Satisfying needs and addressing opportunities:					
● ask people about their preference;					
● recognise that goods are designed, made and distributed;					
● recognise a variety of forms resulting from people's different values, cultures, beliefs and needs;					
● recognise aesthetic qualities in things around them, and use them in their work;					
● recognise that people like certain objects, but not others, find the reason why and use this knowledge in their own designing and appraising;					
● talk about what they have learnt and what they might do differently next time.					
Level 3 Developing and using artefacts, systems and environments In addition pupils working towards level 3 should be taught to:					
● recognise pattern in the structure of objects;					
● know that objects are changed by the forces applied to them;					
● know that systems have inputs, processes and outputs and recognise these in a variety of simple systems;					
● use simple mechanisms to transfer motion;					
● recognise that a source of energy is required to make things work;					
● organise their work, taking account of constraints;					
● realise that, when working in teams, people may have specialist roles;					
● use a variety of energy devices.					

Programme of Study Record Sheet 4	Movement	Changes	Taking Care of Things	Structures	Out and About
Level 3 (continued) Working with materials:					
● recognise that materials and equipment need to be safely stored and maintained;					
● be aware of the dangers of the misuse of materials and equipment, and the consequent risk of accidents;					
● use alternative means of joining materials;					
● recognise the appropriate tools for working with a variety of materials.					
Developing and communicating ideas:					
● develop a range of simple skills used in drawing and modelling.					
Satisfying needs and addressing opportunities:					
● know the importance of exploring needs and opportunities before proposing solutions;					
● recognise that a solution may result in problems in other areas;					
● consider how well their products are designed and made;					
● propose simple modifications to improve the effectiveness of designs and to overcome difficulties when making;					
● reflect, individually and in groups, on how they went about their work, and whether changes might be needed.					